photo by George Holmes, Archer M. Huntington Art Gallery

"Mr. Michener is a born storyteller."
—*The New York Times*

Herein is the beguiling, and very rare, *Collectors, Forgers—and a Writer*, published originally in 1983 in an edition of only 250 copies, with its fascinatingly vivid memories of James Michener's youthful encounters with some of the era's foremost personages in arts and letters. The revealing, introspective, even rarer *Testimony*, originally published in only 200 copies, contains his disclosive *Credo*, enlighteningly informative for the understanding of Michener the writer.

> *I never sought fame's harsh embrace.*
> *I could depart without a trace.*
> *The world owes me no laurels high...*
> *I owe the world.*

"Mr. Michener has become an institution in America."
—*Chicago Tribune*

Older writers are often asked which novels, read when young, influenced them. But since the answer must usually be delivered on the spot and under pressure, a good deal of posing and false recollection results. Now, in sober reflection, I would like to name those books which did actually determine my attitude toward the novel, my style of writing, and my general interpretation of life.

We were an extremely poor family, but each night my hardworking mother assembled the orphan children she took into her home and read to them from the great novelists. So before I could recite the alphabet, I was familiar with Dickens, Thackeray, Reade, and Sienkiewicz. Of these wonderful books, one stands preeminent, *Great Expectations*. It started everything, and I am always pleased when I hear some respectable critic say that he or she considered it a masterpiece. It reminds me that I began at the top.

**By James A. Michener
from Tom Doherty Associates**

*Literary Reflections
My Lost Mexico*

Literary
REFLECTIONS

JAMES A. MICHENER

A TOM DOHERTY ASSOCIATES BOOK
NEW YORK

NOTE: If you purchased this book without a cover you should be aware that this book is stolen property. It was reported as "unsold and destroyed" to the publisher, and neither the author nor the publisher has received any payment for this "stripped book."

LITERARY REFLECTIONS

Copyright © 1993 by James A. Michener
Reprinted by arrangement with State House Press

All rights reserved, including the right to reproduce this book, or portions thereof, in any form.

A Forge Book
Published by Tom Doherty Associates, Inc.
175 Fifth Avenue
New York, N.Y. 10010

Forge® is a registered trademark of Tom Doherty Associates, Inc.

ISBN: 0–812–55052–8

First Forge edition: November 1994

Printed in the United States of America

0 9 8 7 6 5 4 3 2 1

Table of Contents

Introduction...vii

An Emerging Writer 1

   Collectors, Forgers—and a Writer:
   A Memoir 3

   Testimony 93

   Who Is Virgil T. Fry? 131

Verses to a Writer Heading for Ninety...151

Opinions on Other Writers 161

   Ernest Hemingway...............................163

   Margaret Mitchell..................................199

   Marcus Goodrich....................................225

   Truman Capote 265

Sonnet to a Weathered Wanderer...........287

photo by Tim Boole

Introduction

Although I have spent much of the last seven or eight decades reflecting on the literary question of what makes a writer tick, I have not yet arrived at a comprehensive answer. The complex question requires further study. I do know, however, that the process of becoming a writer neither begins nor culminates with the publication of a book; instead it begins in early childhood and persists as long as the writer continues to peck out works on a typewriter or, more likely today, to inject words into a processor.

In recent years I have assumed the pleasant task of trying to teach aspiring writers the secrets of their would-be trade, and this has forced me to recall the processes by which I learned. Over the decades I've analyzed hundreds, perhaps even thousands, of the literary masters, near masters, and never-to-be masters, dissecting their styles and probing their techniques. What did they do to make their writing sing? What mistakes did they make which doomed them to failure? By this means I discovered elements which I could adopt to form my own style and technique, or avoid because, although they might suit some other writer as if invented for him or her, for me they wouldn't work.

In this process I was tempted to do two things: identify what seemed to be general beliefs about writing; and analyze my specific reactions to certain of my contemporaries. This present book is a compilation of my writing in those two veins, and I am delighted that my reflections as a younger man will now be available to other writers.

In *Testimony*, published in 1983 but in an edition of only two hundred copies, I wrote a credo of writing by which I still abide, but I also said several things which I must amend. I wrote: 'I have always thought of myself as a freak . . . who had the great good fortune to stumble into precisely the style of writing for which my personality and education fitted me.' This statement is not fair to me or any writer. None of us 'stumbles into a style of writing.' In trying to teach others, I see that style is a function of study and work, evaluation and work, more study and work, re-evaluation, and more work. Even though I have been publishing for half a century, I still consider myself an emerging writer requiring self-evaluation, study and work. I have made errors during my career, but the only 'fortunate stumble' I took was as a youth employed by the Strath Haven Inn at Swarthmore. If I had not failed to awaken one of the guests in time to catch his train I might have ended up an innkeeper.

I also wrote in that 1983 publication that I thought I was approaching the end of my writing career, but in "The Old Apple Tree," my prologue to *The Eagle and The Raven* (1990), I described the rusty nails that had been driven into my trunk in the nineteen-eighties, goading me back into production. Almost miraculously I have been granted the opportunity to continue to produce—to write—and will continue to do so as long as my eyes can make out the keys on my old typewriter, as long as I can maneuver a finger to peck at those keys, and as long as I retain a mind that can evaluate, study and work. Whether or not my public will continue to stay with me that long is irrelevant, although I'm deeply grateful that they have continued up to now.

Rereading these earlier writings, I am struck by the innumerable factors which helped shape me: writers as varied as Grace Livingston Hill and Truman Capote, with styles as varied as Ernest Hemingway and Sigrid Undset. Every book I've ever read has influenced me. Much of my style, and indeed much of my personality, has been shaped by the poetry I revere. Psychologically as a person and stylistically as a writer I prefer Keats to Shelley, and Wordsworth to Byron. I cherish the poetry of Milton. My own forte is prose, but my homage to the poets occasionally leads me on forays into their métier. In college I began a still-and-never-to-be-finished verse play on Thomas

Chatterton, Wordsworth's 'marvelous boy' who wrote wonderful poetry before his tragic death at age eighteen, and here in *Literary Reflections* are two of my rondeaux, an ode and a sonnet.

I am usually pleased to be asked to comment, in a foreword or introduction, upon the work of another writer, because when the work is good I delight in the opportunity to say so, but also because I can use the opportunity to evaluate how the writer has influenced my own style. In these reflections, again I am struck with the eloquent sparsity of Hemingway, the extraordinary readability of Margaret Mitchell, the simile and metaphor of Marcus Goodrich, and the talent and choice of vocabulary of Capote, whose flair for the bon mot in both his writings and conversations I have always envied and whose life exemplified the fact that artists often require a special freedom. Their style may not be mine, but I've learned from them and their fellows. When I read one of their good books, or even when I merely hold one in my hands, I am made aware of our mutual heritage—our living language which has been used to such wonderful effect by a long and unbroken chain of writers. It is a chain in which I am proud to have forged a small link. What a splendid contribution to our lives a book can be! May the chain of writers be endless.

AN EMERGING WRITER

◇

COLLECTORS,
FORGERS—AND A WRITER:
A MEMOIR

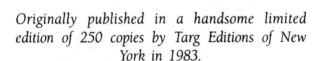

Originally published in a handsome limited edition of 250 copies by Targ Editions of New York in 1983.

photo courtesy of Virginia Trumbull

James A. Michener at Swarthmore College

One

When I was an impecunious student at Swarthmore, a village west of Philadelphia, in the autumn of 1928, we held a mock election at the Quaker college, during which I gave a fiery impromptu speech from the floor defending religious liberty and claiming that Quaker students had every right to vote for the Catholic Al Smith against our fellow-Quaker Herbert Hoover.

My inflamed oratory impressed my classmates not at all; the final straw vote was something like 307 for Hoover and 41 for Smith. But the zest with which I spoke did strike a listener from the town as more or less inspired, and two days later he sought me out. He was Frank Scheibley, a staunch Republican and the proprietor of a famous hostelry in Swarthmore, the Strath Haven Inn, whose kitchen staffed by all blacks including the white-gloved waiters was well regarded throughout the area.

'That was a notable speech thee gave,' Mr. Scheibley said as we sat in my dormitory room. 'Thee has the makings of a fine Republican, and I wonder. . . .'

I pointed out that I had spoken on behalf of the Democratic candidate, and he said jovially: 'Young men of promise always start out as Democrats, but if they find any sense they quickly become Republicans. We rule the nation, you know.'

He was so eager to convert me that on the spot he invited me to drive in to Philadelphia next day and take lunch with him at the formidable Union League Club on Broad Street, and when we were seated in those austere and rather handsome environs, he told me in a low, guarded voice: 'You are probably the only Democrat who will be inside these walls this week.' After a lunch of grand simplicity, he led me upstairs to the library, where portraits of famous Republicans looked down in avuncular grace and there, in a setting calculated to awe anyone, he gave me terrific news: 'James, I've been looking into thy history, and thee needs a father as badly as I need a son. I want thee to come work for me, and in time, who knows, thee could well inherit my inn.'

In this way, I became night watchman at the fine old inn, a rambling wooden structure about which, at nineteen well-selected spots, large metal keys were hung from small metal boxes in such a manner that they could be inserted into a time clock which the watchman carried suspended by a chain from his belt. When properly jammed home, the key imprinted a mark on a slowly revolving tape, showing the exact minute at which contact had been made.

Thus, if I did my job correctly and reached each of the keys at the proper moment, two good results would ensue: I would have inspected every corner of the wooden hotel once each hour to detect fire; and in the morning the manager could check my tape to assure himself that I had done my job properly. It was a system devised by insurance companies who also inspected the tapes

periodically to be certain that the various ho-
tels on which they carried insurance had
been properly guarded against fire.

For the last two years of my college life,
while I was getting summa cum laude
grades in the daytime, I worked all night at
the Strath Haven Inn, reading incessantly in
the waits between my rounds and making
my wonder-filled acquaintance with Stendhal, Flaubert, Dostoyevski, Samuel Butler,
and Fielding.

More important, as it proved, at dawn
each day during one semester I greeted a
gentleman I will call Mr. Kempton who was
staying at the Inn temporarily while his
house in town was being refurbished. He
was about forty-eight, I judged, a quiet, reserved man who enjoyed one of the best occupations in the world, in my opinion. He
was a book publisher, associated with the
prestigious Philadelphia firm of J.B. Lippincott, well regarded for its sober, respectable list and for the cleverness with which
that list was promoted and sold. I could in
those days imagine few occupations more
glamorous than his, and even in later years
when I became a similar executive for a

much larger publisher, the Macmillan Company of New York, I still looked with automatic respect at any book published by Lippincott; they were a Quaker firm and that guaranteed respectability if not daring. Indeed, one of the happiest days of my life came many, many years later when Lippincott actually published one of my books. Had Mr. Kempton then been alive, he would have been proud.

Like Mr. Scheibley, he took me under his wing, and during our brief meetings revealed many interesting facets of the publishing trade. He told me how manuscripts were located, how publishers worked with their authors, and how books finally came into being. One evening he even let me have a handful of galleys, which I carried about the halls with me through the night as I punched my nineteen keys into my belt-suspended clock.

I remember those galleys well, the first I had ever seen or even known about; they were for a romance written by Grace Livingston Hill, a woman about whom I knew nothing but who obviously wrote in a style somewhat removed from Stendhal and

Tolstoy. I was so obviously fascinated by this brush with immortality, this actual handling of a book-about-to-become-a-book, that when I returned the galleys at breakfast to Mr. Kempton he must have been aware of how exciting that night had been for me.

'Thee ought to meet Mrs. Hill,' he said.

'Oh, I'd like that! Would I come in to Philadelphia?' I supposed that I could catch an early morning ride with the Strath Haven truck which went into the city each day to buy fresh produce for the black cooks, but Mr. Kempton said that would be unnecessary: 'Mrs. Hill lives here in Swarthmore.'

For several days I was quite captivated by the realization that a living author shared my village with me, and I even went so far as to look up in the telephone directory where this august lady lived and then walked down to inspect her house from the outside.

It was a distinguished building, set well back from one of those lovely, quiet streets of our Quaker village. It had a driveway leading to the front door which was itself a rather massive affair, and curtains carefully drawn over the eight or ten windows which faced the street. It was neither forbidding nor inviting and seemed the kind of proper house in which the town banker or the most successful doctor would live.

Some days later, as I finished my nightly rounds and greeted Mr. Kempton as he came down to breakfast—we help ate in the kitchen, and very well, too—he said hurriedly: 'James, I've spoken to Mrs. Hill and she'd be delighted to meet thee on Thursday. I'll pick thee up here at the hotel. Four o'clock, and it'll be rather formal.'

This meant full suit, with vest if possible, clean shirt, polished shoes and neatly knotted tie. Mr. Kempton must have left Lippincott early, for he was back at the hotel by three, and I noticed that he was just as careful with his dress as I was with mine, except that his suit hung a little more gracefully from his slight shoulders than mine did from my more shapeless ones.

Since Mrs. Hill lived not far from the Inn, we walked through a fine winter's afternoon, reaching her driveway at precisely four, as planned: 'Remember, James, she is a great lady. One of the greatest.'

Knocking at the door, we waited primly until a black servant opened it to welcome us graciously. We were shown into what we called the parlor, but I noticed that it was much less florid than the parlors of the Dutch farmhouses with which I was familiar, those dour, reserved centers of dark plush used only on Sundays. This was a sunny room with ordinary, comfortable furniture. The black servant told us to sit down, but we were both afraid to do so, lest Mrs. Hill come sweeping into the room, so we stood chatting idly, and it occurred to me that Mr. Kempton was no less nervous than I.

Finally there was a flurry in the hallway outside the room, the door was swung open by the servant, and a woman in her late fifties, I judged, came graciously into the parlor, offered her hand almost eagerly to Mr. Kempton, then turned and faced me: 'So this is the young man who does so well in his studies!' She extended both hands and led me to a chair.

I was to meet Mrs. Hill only twice, this first time with Mr. Kempton, who was her representative at Lippincott, and again later in the year when she invited me to a spring tea at which only she and I were present. On both occasions I found her a delightful hostess, a reserved and somewhat reticent conversationalist, and a woman obviously in love with the work she did and proud of her accomplishments.

It was from Mr. Kempton, at later meetings, that I discovered what those rather remarkable accomplishments were: 'The woman is a phenomenon. She writes an October book for us every year, and sometimes a May one as well. We don't sell the October book in the normal way, that is through bookstores and advertising in *The Bulletin*. No, we publish the book and simply mail it to that extremely faithful circle of readers who buy everything she writes.'

When I looked more fully into the matter I found that what Mr. Kempton said was not only true but also a guarded evaluation. Grace Livingston Hill, this quiet lady living unostentatiously on a quiet street in a quiet Quaker village, was a publishing miracle. Year after year, as regularly as drops falling in the Chinese water torture, books fell from her prolific pen, to be mailed out by Lippincott to the faithful, and year after year about eleven thousand copies of each new title were sold, never fifteen thousand, and never, God forbid, seven thousand. She was a staple, regular as sunrise, the deeply loved mistress of the romantic novel before that genre had been established, the prime practitioner of the semi-gothic before that genre had been defined.

One list of her books contained sixty-one titles, and a mere recitation of a dozen chosen at random indicates that Mrs. Hill was strongest when writing about young women who venture out into the world, who are pursued by evil older men, and who fall in love with the clean, honest lad in the shipping department:

A Girl to Come Home To
The Girl of the Woods
The Prodigal Girl
The Honor Girl
Amorelle
Ladybird

Bright Arrows
Crimson Roses
April Gold
The Enchanted Barn
The Red Signal
Miranda

There were two titles which indicated that occasionally Mrs. Hill grappled with more complicated themes: *The Finding of Jasper Holt* and *The Obsession of Victoria Gracen.*

During my second visit Mrs. Hill, whom I liked very much indeed, for she not only served good refreshments but was also obviously interested in what I was doing, gave me two of her books. This produced some problems, for as I remember my junior year of honors work at Swarthmore, that was the period during which I first read *Madame Bovary* and *Vanity Fair*, and like any young man of good sense, I was passionately in love with Emma and Becky, two young women rather more spirited than any I knew personally. Therefore, Mrs. Hill's two American heroines, whose names I do not remember, stood in rather strong contrast to the two European women, and I recall thinking several times: 'Why doesn't somebody shake Mrs. Hill's heroines?'

I was also put off by her girls' extreme religiosity, because this was characteristic in all of Mrs. Hill's books, and accounted, Mr. Kempton said, for her popularity with so many readers. For me, at age twenty and filled with Kant, Nietzsche and Ibsen, it was somewhat cloying, so that whereas I liked

15

M ANY thousands of readers have found inspiration and happiness in reading the novels of Grace Livingston Hill. In her charming romances there is a sympathetic buoyant spirit that conquers discouragement, which trusts that true love and happiness will come out of the worst trial. Hers is the priceless gift of understanding and it is that quality that makes her stories so true to life and her people real.

Grace Livingston Hill's

novels are as thoroughly modern as they are wholesome and refreshing ⌐

AMORELLE
APRIL GOLD
ARIEL CUSTER
BEAUTY FOR ASHES
THE BELOVED STRANGER
THE BEST MAN
BLUE RUIN
THE CHALLENGERS
THE CHANCE OF A LIFETIME
THE CHRISTMAS BRIDE
THE CITY OF FIRE
CLOUDY JEWEL
COMING THROUGH THE RYE
CRIMSON ROSES
DAWN OF THE MORNING
DUSKIN
THE ENCHANTED BARN
EXIT BETTY
THE FINDING OF JASPER HOLT
FOUND TREASURE
THE GIRL FROM MONTANA
THE GOLD SHOE
HAPPINESS HILL
THE HONOR GIRL
JOB'S NIECE
KERRY
LADYBIRD
LO, MICHAEL!
THE MAN OF THE DESERT

MARCIA SCHUYLER
MATCHED PEARLS
MIRANDA
MYSTERY FLOWERS
THE MYSTERY OF MARY
A NEW NAME
NOT UNDER THE LAW
THE OBSESSION OF
          VICTORIA GRACEN
OUT OF THE STORM
THE PATCH OF BLUE
PHOEBE DEANE
THE PRODIGAL GIRL
RAINBOW COTTAGE
THE RANSOM
RE-CREATIONS
THE RED SIGNAL
THE SEARCH
SILVER WINGS
THE STORY OF A WHIM
THE STRANGE PROPOSAL
TOMORROW ABOUT THIS TIME
THE TRYST
A VOICE IN THE WILDERNESS
THE WHITE FLOWER
THE WHITE LADY
WHITE ORCHIDS
THE WITNESS

GROSSET & DUNLAP   *Publishers*   NEW YORK

Back cover of one of Grace Livingston
Hill's books

Mrs. Hill very much, and stood in awe of her as the first professional writer with whom I had come into contact, I forswore her novels and followed her career thereafter only from a distance.

My relationship with my first editor ended poorly, too. One night at eleven Mr. Kempton told me: 'James, I have a most important meeting tomorrow in New York. Thee must call me at six so that I can catch the early train to West Philadelphia.'

I must have been reading some fascinating book that night because I clean forgot the six o'clock calls, and at close to seven Mr. Kempton came storming down demanding to know why he had not been called. I was sitting at the switchboard at the time, having finished my six o'clock rounds and not yet starting on my seven when he roared up, took one look at me, dismissed me with disgust and darted out to catch a taxi in which to overtake his commuter train at some station down the line.

We were never close after that. He took me to Mrs. Hill's no more, and as spring wound down he returned to his own home, now refinished, from where he continued to look after the affairs of Grace Livingston Hill. Once when I mentioned her name to some visitors from Philadelphia, a man who knew the publishing industry said: 'Lippincotts ought to encase her in gold and hide her in their safe. She keeps the company solvent.' That autumn and through all the autumns that I knew of her, she presented to her adoring public one of her full length, well crafted, romantic-religious novels, and she was still going strong both when I left the area to study in Europe and when I returned. She was an inexhaustible fountain of sentimental romances: *Job's Niece, The Patch of Blue, Sunrise.*

Many critics, if casual readers can be accorded that exalted title, have felt that Grace Livington Hill's chef d'oeuvre is a somewhat longer novel she published for the 1936 distribution, because *Mystery Flowers* combines her many strengths and displays her major themes to good advantage.

The novel opens with an engaging scene. 'Diana Disston,' young and pretty of course, 'stood at the window watching for the postman.' She is perplexed by what waits at her elbow: 'a tall crystal bud vase with three pink carnations.'

Sweet flowers! So mysterious and lovely. Coming in such a magical way ... one every morning in her path just where she went down the driveway to take her daily walk ... A single perfect bloom lying in almost the same spot every morning! It couldn't have *happened*. Not three times just alike!

Diana, of course, is in trouble. Her mother has died before the novel begins and in the first few pages her father announces that he is going to remarry, and he has chosen as his second wife one of the most objectionable bitches of that period, whose character is defined obliquely in the paragraph relating how Diana reacts to the news:

'Oh, *not* Cousin Helen!' she gasped aloud in quivering sobs, shuddering as she wept. 'Oh, he can't he *can't*—he *wouldn't* do that! My f-f-father—w-w-wouldn't—do *thha-at!*'

So Stepmother Helen invades the big house, treats Diana abominably in secret and fools everybody except the faithful Scottish maid, Maggie, who sees through her immediately:

> 'Men is that stupid when it comes to judgin' a pretty wumman, especially if she had a bright way with her and knows how ta work her eyes. Ah! but the puir mon'll rue the day he ever saw her . . .'

Diana's only hope of escape from the dismal house ruled by the awful Helen stems from the fact that she is being ardently courted by a local lad, Mr. Bobby Watkins, one of the sorriest rich drips of the 1930s. 'She could have anything she wanted if she belonged to him.' But he was such a pathetic character, boastful on the one hand, cringing on the other, that she knew she had to escape that marriage.

Fortunately she was also being courted by Arthur McWade: 'He was a nice kind man, but very formal in spite of his brilliant intellect. Diana always felt rather overpowered in his company.'

———

So there you have the plot, all laid forth by page 31 of a 232-page novel with a mysterious perfect flower arriving from nowhere at each critical moment in the story. There is, however, one other major character.

In the little stone cottage which guarded the great iron gates of the Disston mansion lives a poor Scottish widow, Mrs. MacCarroll, with her son Gordon, tall, handsome, rugged, loyal, helpful to his mother and above all a devout, trustworthy Christian. The reader can probably guess who it is who has been leaving the single perfect flowers where the distraught Diana can find them.

By a truly ingenious twist of plot the Disstons in the big house are not aware that the MacCarrolls, mother and son, are living in the gate cottage: 'It had been rented through an agent, and the new tenants had moved in without the family in the big house even knowing they were there.' And so the interesting involvements of the novel are free to develop.

Mrs. Hill was never averse to slipping into her romances scenes of hot sexuality, as when Mr. Bobby Watkins reveals himself for the monster he is:

> His hot breath was upon her face, and his thick moist lips suddenly pressed possessively upon hers, as if he would draw her very soul from her body in a kiss that suddenly became to her repulsive, unclean. His eyes looking into hers in the moonlight had the selfish beastly look of a cannibal about to sate his cruel desire for human blood.

What awful thing had Mr. Bobby Watkins done? He had tried to kiss her at the sacred spot in the roadway where the mystery flowers appeared each day.

Beset on all sides, poor Diana can do nothing but quit her father's house, and as she flees down the lane one dark night a scene develops which has been described as one of the most effective Mrs. Hill was ever to write. Through a device which is never made clear, the fleeing girl hears a mysterious man praying; it is, of course, Gordon MacCarroll, though why he should be praying on the opposite side of the hedge at near midnight is not explained:

> 'And Lord we would ask Thy mercy and tenderness and leading for the people up at the great house. Perhaps some of them are sad, Lord, give them comfort. Perhaps they need Thy guidance. Do Thou send Thy light—!'

Now Diana has two crutches in the difficult days ahead, the flowers and the prayer, and surely she needs them, for the days prove very difficult indeed. From page 81 to 208 she experiences various torments in the city as she tries vainly to earn a respectable living. Her landlady is an ogre. Her diet is a glass of milk daily plus one little packet of peanut butter sandwiches. Almost starving because Stepmother Helen has bullied Diana's father into terminating her allowance, she takes a job addressing envelopes in a publisher's offices but this does not last long. A pleasant oaf named Jerry Lange tried to make love to her, in the 1936-sense of holding hands, but she rebuffs him, and when it seems that life has run its course for this beautiful nineteen-year-old girl, two things happen.

Mysteriously, out of nowhere, a young woman hands Diana a tract HE UNDER-STANDS! and this brings her to Jesus; and equally mysteriously a large box arrives from a florist's. When she opens it, she sees 'Carnations. Myriads of them! Her mystery flowers had come to find her!' Emotionally she is stabilized, but economically she is in such disastrous straits that she must take a job as waitress in a cheap restaurant, where all sorts of dismal things happen to her, but at the depth of each depression, the mysterious flowers arrive from this person she has not yet met: 'Flowers! *Precious* flowers!'

Meanwhile, at the Disston mansion things have deteriorated. Stepmother Helen has taken up with an unsavory character, Max Copley, who has a yacht, Mr. Disston teeters on the edge of bankruptcy, and it is obvious that some climax must be reached to solve these various dilemmas. The wicked stepmother must be gotten ride of; Mr. Disston's fortunes must be resuscitated; and Diana must discover who it is who has been sending her the mystery flowers.

Mrs. Hill solves her problems rather neatly, I thought. The stepmother runs off with Max Copley on his yacht and a few days later, with no unnecessary explanation a headline appears in what one must assume are the Philadelphia newspapers: YACHT 'LOTUS BLOSSOM' SINKS IN MID-OCEAN WITH ALL ON BOARD! At the same time it is revealed that Diana's grandmother had written a will giving the big house not to the father Stephen Disston but to Diana direct. And of course Diana discovers that the one who sent her the flowers of mystery was the same whom she heard praying beyond the hedge.

A much-chastened Father Disston says, when the young man asks for Diana's hand in marriage: 'There isn't a man in the world that I would as soon trust my girl with as you, Gordon MacCarroll.' As to the fact that Diana is suddenly not a waitress but an heiress to a considerable fortune, Mr. Disston says: 'But this should make no difference to you, Gordon. Money should not enter into the scheme of things when two people love one another. It is only something for which to be thankful when God chooses to send more than you asked.'

In the concluding pages it becomes the opinion of everyone that God has arranged for things to happen as they did, and devout Gordon, no longer a poor young man living in the little gate house, forgives even Step-mother Helen: 'You can't tell what may have happened between her soul and God at the last minute,' when the yacht went down.

'Oh, do you think so?' Diana said, turning eager, longing eyes on her lover. 'Oh, I hope she is saved. I used to hate her, but now I hope she is saved. Since I have learned that Jesus loved everybody enough to die for them I can love her too. And I don't want her to be lost.'

Two

It was a heady experience for a young man who loved literature to meet a professional writer like Grace Livingston Hill, even though upon sober analysis I had to admit that she produced books not exactly comparable to Thomas Hardy's or Sigrid Undset's. It was another literary adventure, however, which had a somewhat more stabilizing influence on me.

I had the good fortune to be an English student of Professor Robert Spiller, a brilliant scholar who was already the world's foremost authority on James Fenimore Cooper and who would soon, after transferring to the University of Pennsylvania, become a moving spirit in the writing of the authoritative history of American literature. I would always be indebted to Dr. Spiller for two unusual contributions to my education. I was a difficult young man, all elbows, all animosity as I strove to find my definitions, and I had been thrown out of every school I had ever attended: primary, junior high, high school and now college, for good reason. But Dr. Spiller told the governing board of the college that no young man who wrote two long term papers in iambic pentameter of a high quality could be all bad, so on his voucher I was allowed back.

Also, at just about this time he found a holograph copy, in the poet's unquestioned handwriting, of a little known poem by William Cowper, and he invited me, at age nineteen I believe it must have been, to help him edit this for publication in the most prestigious scholarly journal of its day, the sacred PMLA (Publication of the Modern Language Association). My first appearance anywhere in serious print, other than poetry and sports writing for a small-town newspaper, was in the top journal of the period, and for this vote of confidence I have always been indebted to Dr. Spiller.

One winter, and it may have been the one preceding my visit to Grace Livingston Hill, Dr. Spiller arranged for his honors class to visit a remarkable man who lived some distance away on The Main Line, and I make a point of this location because we at Swarthmore always had an inferiority complex over the fact that two premier Quaker colleges—at that time—Bryn Mawr for girls and Haverford for boys, were located handsomely on the fashionable Main Line of the omnipotent Pennsylvania Railroad, while trailing Swarthmore was stuck off on a rather shabby affair called, of all things, The Wawa Branch.

There is extant a letter which a famous professor wrote to the young Rhodes Scholar Frank Aydelotte, the man who was about to revolutionize small-college education through his judicious experiments at Swarthmore, warning him that if he accepted the presidency of Swarthmore rather than a job at Haverford he would be committing himself to the second rate, and two of the compelling reasons this professor cited were that Haverford had a much better library and that Swarthmore was stuck away on The Wawa Branch.

It was with a sense of exploration and daring that we country bumpkins from The Wawa Branch rode over one snowy day to invade the sacred confines of The Main Line and out to the pleasant village of Daylesford, where a surprising house awaited us. We had been warned by Dr. Spiller that the owner was 'irascible, a lover of all things English, and very rich.' He was, we had learned from our own researches, sixty-five years old and a veteran of the electrical industry, in which he had amassed his important fortune, a considerable portion of which he had devoted to the collecting of rare first editions and other incunabula.

His house was, as I said, surprising, for we had expected one of those Pennsylvania mansions which had sprouted during the early years of this century when the Pennsylvania Railroad and anthracite coal created vast fortunes, but instead we found a handsome Elizabethan-style shingled house, low and rambling and quite large. It was surrounded by trees which had been planted with obvious care, and gave the impression of being a house in which people lived who enjoyed life.

When the owner appeared to greet us he was dressed in a bright black-and-white hound's-tooth checkered suit of English cut, a stiff wing-tip collar, and a flashy bow tie, but what astonished me was that in all things—from his rotund build to his bright, witty eyes—he resembled Samuel Pickwick. He displayed elegant manners but also a no-nonsense warmth which infected all who came near him; he was an Uncle Toby type of man whom I liked immediately.

He was A. Edward Newton, one of Philadelphia's illuminati, and he had already written a famous book about collecting which had made him notorious throughout literary circles and was in the process of publishing another. A man proud of his accomplishments, he embraced us all, led us into his spacious bookcase-lined living room and launched a long afternoon which none of us who shared it would ever forget. It apparently impressed him as much as it did us, for later he wrote in one of his books:

Some time ago, Professor Spiller of Swarthmore College brought to my home a company of young men and maidens who were 'taking English' under his direction, and I was struck with their keenness and intelligence. . . .

Unfortunately, I was not among those who impressed him favorably, and I failed for a curious reason. I was, of course, bedazzled by his wealth of riches; he had at that time about ten thousand valuable books, including many historic rarities, and I cannot forget the subdued thrill that passed among us when he passed out first editions with dedicatory autographs by Thackeray, Thoreau, Tennyson, George Eliot, Thomas Gray, Hawthorne and Thomas Hardy. It was as if these noble figures had come to join us in the room, and we were awed.

One by one he produced his wonders, distributing them as if they had been copies of this morning's newspaper, and we could see that he was proud of his holdings but not at all pompous as to his temporary custodianship. He treated his treasures as important books, not arcane art objects; they were works to be read and he invited us to read them.

But as he progressed it became clear to me that he was heading down avenues in which I either could not or did not wish to follow. His two great loves were Dr. Samuel Johnson, whom I found to be an arrogant bore who inflated a modest talent into an immodest posturing; and William Blake, whom I did not understand, which made his intellectual vagaries distasteful and bewildering. Therefore, during the long middle part of our visit I did not participate, and when Newton passed around items from his really extraordinary collection of Johnson memorabilia, I politely passed each handful along to my neighbor, a fact which Mr. Newton noticed.

I did the same with what I now acknowledge to have been the great Blake etchings and watercolors; at that time I was not ready for them, and I have never hesitated during my long exploration of the arts to respond honestly to any work as of the moment it was presented to me. Thus I missed Scott Fitzgerald and Thomas Wolfe, Kafka and Klee, Handel and Haydn, Blake and

Coleridge, and I have never apologized for my astigmatism; when the proper time came, often decades later, I was eager to revise my early estimates.

So I had missed the two figures whom Newton prized most, and finally my insolence was too much for him to accept: 'And what does this young scholar prefer?'

There was challenge and irritation in his voice, so on the cutting edge of the moment I made a preposterous reply: 'I'm the kind of person who prefers Keats to Shelley, and Wordsworth to Byron.' This self-analysis still obtains fifty-five years after that first utterance; it remains the best psychological description so far offered.

Its effect on Newton was electrical. Delighted with such capsule definition, he hurried to a kind of vault from which he brought one of the great rarities of English literary history, that exquisite, heartbreaking watercolor sketch which the minor poet Joseph Severn made of the dying John Keats on the dark night of '28th January 1821, 3 o'clock m'g. Drawn to keep me awake—a deadly sweat was on him all this night.'

I held it in my hands, one of the most

cherished portraits in English history, a thing as frail and delicate as the subject it portrayed, and I was struck silent by its reality, its immediacy, its sense of death and the vast sadness which came over the world of poetry when this immortally gifted young man of twenty-six died.

In a pocket of the frame in which the portrait was kept was a handwritten note by Tennyson, proposing a possible text for a memorial to the artist: 'To the memory of Joseph Severn, the devoted friend of John Keats by whose deathbed he watched and whose name he lived to see inscribed among the immortal poets of England.' When Tennyson finished composing these lines he apparently realized that they were elliptical at best and ungrammatical at worst, for he revised the closing part to read, more correctly, 'inscribed among *those of* the immortal poets of England,' and I could visualize Tennyson, seventy-two years old when he wrote the epitaph, secure in the knowledge that he too would find a place among the 'immortal poets of England.'

This combination of two men I respected joining hands in one item so impressed me that I wanted to see all the Keats memorabilia, and Newton had an ample supply: three other good portraits by Severn, a letter to Fanny Brawne, and a sonnet by Rosetti in his handwriting memorializing Keats on the sixtieth anniversary of his, Keats', death.

To be in the presence of so many books once handled by Keats, to hold manuscripts which came from his pen, and to see the letters which attested to his love for Fanny Brawne quite awed me, and when Newton perceived this he asked: 'Can you quote any passages from your favorite poet?' and without hesitating I launched into the lusher passages of *Ode on a Grecian Urn*:

Thou still unravished bride of
    quietness,
Thou foster-child of silence and slow
    time. . . .

What men or gods are these? What
    maidens loth?
What mad pursuit? What struggle to
    escape?
What pipes and timbrels? What wild
    ecstasy. . . .

John Keats

Who are these coming to the sacrifice?
To what green altar, O mysterious priest,
Lead'st thou that heifer lowing at the
skies,
And all her silken flanks with garlands
dressed. . . .

"Beauty is truth, truth beauty,"—that is
all
Ye know on earth, and all ye need to
know.

Newton approved of this exhibition, saying that if a young man had not memorized large passages of poetry by the time he was twenty he had wasted a good portion of his life; then he asked me what my favorite Keats was, and once more without qualification I named a poem from which I had memorized large slabs and which I would read in its entirety at least once each year for the rest of my life; its magical evocation of the Middle Ages enchanted me then as it does still:

St. Agnes Eve—Ah, bitter chill it was!
The owl, for all his feathers, was a-cold;

> The hare limped trembling through the
>   frozen grass,
> And silent was the flock in the woolly
>   fold. . . .

I rattled off some twenty lines, excerpted from various parts of the long poem, and then I said with youthful presumption and complete conviction: 'I often recite to myself one stanza which seems to stand at the heart of the poem. . . .' Then I added, in some embarrassment: 'What I mean is, it throws the narrative forward,' and Newton said: 'I should have thought poetical quality was more important than narrative,' and I replied: 'In a long poem you better have both.'

> So, purposing each moment to retire,
> She lingered still. Meantime across the
>   moors,
> Had come young Porphyro, with heart
>   on fire
> For Madeline. Beside the portal doors,
> Buttressed from moonlight, stands he,
>   and implores
> All saints to give him sight of Madeline,

But for one moment in the tedious
	hours,
That he might gaze and worship all
	unseen;
Perchance speak, kneel, touch, kiss—in
	sooth such things have been.

I think I knew then that within a few years
I would be striding across the moors of
Scotland, my own heart on fire with concepts and imaginings that would fuel my
brain interminably, and I wonder now, after
all these years, how young men are able to
devise plans for the long span of their lives
if they do not know at least some good poetry to recite when they are alone.

As the lovely day waned, Newton turned
abruptly to a curious subject, holding us enthralled as he recounted the adventures of a
famous forger, then living, who had discovered that rich Americans like Newton who
were fascinated by English literature were
easy prey for anyone who could print up a
series of faked first editions.

'This brilliant and engaging man, posing
as a devoted London bookseller, got himself
some old paper, some proper fonts of type

and a trustworthy bookbinder and quietly inserted into the marketplace a series of really choice items. He never attempted anything big and blazing like my Shakespeare Folio,' and here he pointed to that noble volume, 'but he did create the smaller volumes by Keats, Shelley and Byron.' I noticed with regret that the forger apparently thought Wordsworth beneath his attention.

'One of his accomplices tried to fool me with some of the forgeries,' Newton said, 'and I would have tumbled for them. Anyone would, but I have a personal friend in London, one to be trusted on such matters, and he protected me, pointing out the cleverness of the forgeries and how to detect them. He's Thomas J. Wise.' (The reader is advised to note carefully this name, as it will resurface later.)

From the galleys of a book he was about to publish Mr. Newton showed us a rather long passage in which he extolled Mr. Wise's perspicacity, and also a photograph of the great scholar himself, an austere, cautious-looking gentleman in dark suit, pearl stickpin and wing-tipped collar. He wore a

Thomas James Wise

mustache, had a firm lower jaw and piercing eyes; obviously he was a man not to be tampered with:

> Thomas James Wise of London, who is, without doubt, the most learned book-collector we have to-day. He is not a college man; that is to say, he did not study at a college; but as the University of Oxford has honored him with a degree, it will be admitted that he is a scholar.

Newton had in his possession but not in his collection one spectacular forgery which occupied me for the remainder of the afternoon. Actually, it was a forgery of a forgery, which made it doubly interesting, and I remember handling the little volume with an awe that remained with me for many weeks; there was no way by which I could have detected the fraud, and had I been a collector I am sure I would have grabbed at this wonderfully evocative book.

It was the subject matter which mesmerized me, for this book re-created the Bristol forgeries of the inspired boy, Thomas Chatterton, who wrote his first major poem at the age of ten, who constructed an entire medieval world in his imagination, then forged the poems supposed to have been written in a nearby abbey now in ruins, and who starved to death in an attic at eighteen, hastening his death by a heavy dose of arsenic.

For the rest of that year I lay under the spell of Chatterton and started a verse play, to which I would come back a dozen times in later years, depicting the fabled life of this unique lad whom Wordsworth called 'the marvelous boy' and whom both Keats and Shelley praised in major poems. My play, I'm afraid, was filled with cobwebs, bailiffs and medieval stone work, but it was also filled with Chatterton, whose ghost has never completely left me.

I returned once to talk with Newton, finding him just as warm and outgoing when talking to one student as he had been when entertaining sixteen with his stories. He told me, with obvious relish, that some Bryn Mawr girls had been by to see his collection and that one of them had perched on his knee, giving him a kiss as she said: 'You look just like my grandfather.' When I asked him how he had responded he replied: 'I told her, "Lassie, you'll grow tired of this long before I will." '

I told him I wanted to see his Chatterton forgery, but he said he'd returned it long since, and then he heckled me about my preference for Wordsworth, trying to ascertain whether I really knew anything about him, and in his challenging way he asked: 'Can you recite anything from him?'

The first serious poem I had ever memorized was Milton's sonnet *On His Blindness*, but I also knew some of Wordsworth's *Tintern Abbey* and snatches of two other sonnets, which I recited. The poem I liked best I saved till last, *Intimations of Immortality*. I could not begin to recite all of it, but I had in the first days of my study of this congenial poet memorized the stanza beginning 'Our birth is but a sleep and a forgetting . . .' and when shortly I reached the deeply moving lines I could see Newton nodding agreement.

Not in entire forgetfulness,
And not in utter nakedness,

But trailing clouds of glory do we come
From God who is our home:
Heaven lies about us in our infancy!
Shades of the prison house begin to
    close
Upon the growing boy,
But he beholds the light, and whence it
    flows. . . .

I did not have the courage to tell Dr. Newton about my designs for a play about Chatterton, but I suppose he must have known that I had developed a more than passing interest in the young Bristol poet, and we spent some time discussing his curious life.

As we talked I spoke of my enormous respect for Matthew Arnold and he laughed: 'You really like prose, don't you?' and I told him that I thought Wordsworth, Milton and Arnold, my three great favorites that year, were very fine poets, but he explained: 'They're not lyric poets. They write prose in verse form.' This was too complex for me to grasp at that point in my education, so I said no more in defense of my poets and refused to concede that they were in any way lesser figures than Keats, Shelley and Byron, but after many decades of pondering the problem I did one day exclaim: 'At last I understand what Newton was arguing. I do love my preferred poets because they write prose, putting it in poetic form, and I believe that's why they're so completely wonderful.' Much of my adult attitude toward prose would stem from my early study and memorization of long passages from Wordsworth and Milton and from my grave respect for Arnold.

In the years following that second meeting I watched Newton's career with admiration; he consolidated his position as America's foremost bibliophile, defended cultural activities and achieved for himself a distinguished role in belles-lettres. In fact, his career paralleled that of Dr. Spiller, as each man attained for himself an enviable reputation, and I have often considered myself fortunate to have known at a malleable age two men of such outstanding achievement. They formed an excellent pair of cicerones into the world of letters.

Several years before Newton died an explosive little book was published under a deceptively simple title which masked its revolutionary character: *An Enquiry into the Nature of Certain Nineteenth Century Pamphlets*, by John Carter and Graham Pollard. The pamphlets in question were noble items of English literature which the staid, pompous London bibliophile Thomas J. Wise had forged with a subtle skill that deceived the experts. I was sorry that Newton had not been spared the shameful uncovering of his friend, for I recalled a tribute he had written about the great forger:

> Indeed I may say that until I saw, and saw repeatedly, Mr. Wise's books I had no idea that it was possible to secure so many volumes in such faultless condition.

When Newton's own collection was put up for sale at Parke-Bernet in 1941, half a year after his death, finicky experts complained that many of his choicest items were no better than 'cripples,' the designation for books which were unquestionably authentic but in such abominable condition that no serious collector would want them. One such expert has written:

In the course of his stay [in San Francisco] he visited my bookshop and gave me a half hour lecture on the importance of buying only fine copies of books. I never saw a worse case of someone not practising what he preached. When I got to New York I was warned by my bookseller friends there that I was going to be disappointed in Newton's library, but I had to see the books to believe them. I viewed the first sale with some gloom. At least sixty percent of the lots I wanted to bid on were in such poor condition that I scratched them off my list.

No one could castigate Thomas J. Wise on the condition of *his* collection; he filled it with books of pristine cleanliness which he himself had printed.

In the 1970s, when Newton was long-since dead and I was working on the Eastern Shore of Maryland, I was forcibly reminded of him by a bizarre experience. At three different cocktail parties along the Chesapeake, which was then the focus of my attention, well meaning friends said: 'Jim, you ought to see the library that Arthur Houghton has in his house at Wye Plantation.' I had heard of both Houghton, a former executive of Corning Glass who had given a great library at Harvard University, and of his rather massive establishment at Wye River, but no one had ever specified why his personal library was worth seeing, so I supposed it was some unusually fine bit of walnut paneling with movable ladders like the one shown in the famous trademark of Leary's Bookstore on Market Street in Philadelphia, in which an eighteenth-century bibliophile stands atop a ladder to reach the highest shelf of his library.

I took no steps to see such architecture, but one afternoon a duck-hunting neighbor with the unfortunate nickname of Dago told me: 'Arthur Houghton's stopping by tonight, and I want you to meet him. You must see his library.' Dago Springs had received his name at Princeton where, to save money during a bleak spell, the college dining hall had served spaghetti one night a week; the other students abhorred it, but to their surprise young Springs, whose family owned one of the great spinning mills in New England, not only liked it but preferred it: 'I used to clean the platter. Delicious. So they started calling me Dago and it stuck.'

When I reported to Dago's delightful house on the point, surrounded by nesting places for heron and coves in which Canada geese abounded, I met in *his* library a tall, austere, distinguished man who looked as if he had just stepped out of the middle pages of a John Marquand novel—the scene in which the hero comes home from Harvard to meet his formidable father. But our first moments of conversation dispelled any such interpretation of the man, for on prompting from my wife he launched into one of the damnedest love stories of recent history:

'Yes, Mrs. Michener, what you ask about is true. I was living in Florida and my wife-to-be, Nina Rodale over there, was living about two miles away. We had never met, and probably never would have, for we were engaged in much different pursuits.

'Nina was an oceanographer interested in sea lions, and unknown to me she had more or less tamed this one beast who liked to leave her pool and wander about the shore. One afternoon I received a telephone call from the police. Would I look to see if there was a sea lion in my swimming pool? I thought this a most unusual interrogation, but I went out to the yard and there, sure enough, was this sea lion splashing about and making himself at home.

'Some time later, this very attractive young woman appeared at my door with a station wagon and helpers to catch her sea lion and take him home.

'Well, on two subsequent occasions her sea lion came trundling up to spend time in my pool, and on each occasion when she came to fetch him she impressed me just as much as her sea lion had done, and so we got married.'

My wife asked the obvious question: 'Did you ever suspect that she had trained her sea lion where to stop for his siesta?' and he confessed that the idea had sometimes crossed his mind.

Nina Houghton was of double interest to me, for I had known her father rather well, J.I. Rodale, the health-food fanatic of Emmaus, a small German settlement not far from where I lived in Pennsylvania. I had listened attentively to Rodale's lecturing on food and I attributed much of my unusual energy to the fact that I have more or less followed his advice on certain matters like vitamins and roughage in the diet. I thought it most appropriate when he died on camera at the height of a Dick Cavett television show on which he was advocating good eating habits and lots of exercise if one wanted to enjoy a long life. He was in advanced years when he toppled over in front of millions . . . a flawless Rodale performance one of my friends said.

But my indebtedness to Rodale goes much deeper than that. Late in life, like almost every writer I know, he got fed up with trying to find synonyms in *Roget's Thesaurus*, one of the most brilliant and unusable books in English. Every young writer grabs hold of a copy, and almost no one ever

learns how to use it effectively, for the orga-
nization is beyond the mastery of an ordinary intelligence. I quickly learned, in Dr.
Spiller's fine class on research—and am I
glad I received an A in *that* one—that if I
sought a synonym for the word *true*, I was
required, by *Roget*, to take a course in the
philosophy of the concept *true* in all its
manifestations and shadings, and that by
the time I found the simple substitute I was
seeking, half an hour at least had passed. I
was about to say that the half hour had been
wasted, but that of course would not be accurate; the time was never wasted, for one
did learn something about the intricacies of
this word, but he rarely found the synonym
he was seeking.

Most writers are simple-minded folk; they
do not require a course in apologetics when
they seek a mere substitute, and it was
Rodale's brilliant discovery of this fact
which led him to make a revealing calcula-
tion, which one of his staff explained:

'The boss took a *Roget* and studied it,
and what he found was that a huge
amount of space was wasted in the

index. If you organize your book on the *Roget* principle and want it to be functional, you must provide a massive index. His genius decision was simple. Do away with the index altogether.

'And with the space thus saved he'd have ample room to print all his words in one grand alphabetical sequence.

'See how wonderfully usable it becomes. Up front you enter *audacious*, and then you give some seventy synonyms, not in a general hodge-podge but arranged under the three principal extensions of the word: *courageous*, *foolhardy*, *impudent*. Then, when you reach *courageous*, you enter all its synonyms, including of course *audacious*.

'But the overlap is not as great as you might suspect, because the word *audacious* embraces certain subtleties of meaning which *courageous* does not have, and vice versa. And you do the same with all the other synonyms of both words, so that what you have is a wonderful interlocking system of words and meanings.

'To appreciate the beauty of this simplicity let's look at this page with the word *true*. Here you have a separate indented heading for each of its seven different meanings: *authentic* has 13 synonyms; *correct* 25; *legitimate* 9; *veracious* 14; *faithful* 15; *honest* 15; and *straight* 13. That makes a total of 104 synonyms for *true*.

'But see what a beautiful web this system weaves. When you cross-check on the word *authentic* in its major entry you find two major definitions with a total of 43 synonyms, one of which, of course, is *true*. And when you check *honest* you find that it has five differentiated meanings with so many total entries I won't try to count them.

'To use Rodale's *Synonym Finder* is to play with words the way Beethoven played with a piano. Most serious professional writers use it, because it's a professional tool.'

I discounted the Rodale man's claim that most professional writers use the new thesaurus as home-office boasting, but I will say three things about the book. (1) I have never known a professional writer intelligent enough to use *Roget*. (2) I have been thanked by many professionals to whom I've introduced the Rodale version. (3) Bill Safire, the *New York Times*' resident lexicographer, has signed a blurb which applies about a dozen superlative adjectives to his Rodale, and I can think of several he missed.

So I was more than pleased to pay my respects to Rodale's daughter; I did not expect much from her husband's library; I assumed it was one of those fumed-oak things with an *Oxford Dictionary* and a set of Thomas Hardy.

When I drove up to the Houghtons' Georgian mansion I had second thoughts; so beautiful was the estate on one of the loveliest backwaters of the Chesapeake Bay, and so delightfully proportioned the grounds with their peacocks that I told my wife: 'This place really could have a library.' But when I was taken into it, I saw that it was indeed what I had feared: a small room, well-paneled with one original Rembrandt and about eighty well-bound books. And that was it.

However, after lunch, with the peacocks parading across the stately eighteenth-century garden, Arthur Houghton said diffidently: 'Should we, perhaps, stop by to see the library?' I nodded, supposing that one of the books I'd overlooked was a Shakespeare *Folio* or a first edition of Swinburne.

He led me right past the little library, out the front door, and across the lawn to a splendid two-story Georgian building as big as a large-sized cottage, and inside the front door he said: 'Left or right? On the left I have an interesting collection, and over there I have my manuscripts.' I chose the right, and we entered a very large room whose walls were entirely covered with bookcases, each linear foot of which was filled with treasures.

'You know books,' Houghton said, stepping back to see what I would take down. I spent some minutes just surveying the riches without being able to decipher any of the titles, and I judged that I was looking at more than a thousand apparently precious items.

By the sheerest chance the item I took down was one which I might well have chosen had I consulted an index: the original manuscript of Gilbert White's immortal essay on the country beauties of England and one of the world's first ecological studies: *The Natural History and Antiquities of Selborne.* In my own writings I have been much influenced by any physical setting in which I found myself, and this preoccupation has stemmed in part from my early love for *Selborne,* and by William Cobbett's *Rural Rides,* in which an intelligent countryman in the early years of the nineteenth century simply rode through the back roads of England and reported what he saw.

Now, to hold the pages from which White had built his splendid book was an excitement for which I had not been prepared, and then to pass at random among this extraordinary collection of books and to find the original manuscripts of Elizabeth Barrett Browning's love letters to Robert and her haunting *Sonnets from the Portuguese* was something I could never have anticipated, and I was astonished to find, in a building so close to my home in the rural backwaters of Maryland, the personal papers of Samuel Pepys and the manuscript of Alexander Pope's earliest surviving work, and off in one corner the complete manuscript of Arnold Toynbee's studies in history . . . this was adventuring.

My eye kept coming back to that tall and somewhat ungainly volume published by Jaggard and Blount in 1623, the one book which contains perhaps more of man's incandescent brilliance than any other ever printed: the folio edition of *Mr. William Shakespeare's Comedies, Histories & Tragedies*. How impoverished we would have been had this book never been published.

But what gave me special pleasure that day was to discover that several of Houghton's particular treasures had been acquired at the public dispersal of the A. Edward Newton collection in 1941. These separate little books of poems by

Carew, Lovelace and Meredith had all been Newton's, and I might have lifted into my hands during one of my visits to Daylesford this delightful manuscript of the novel Charlotte Brontë had written at the age of eighteen.

And thinking of Newton reminded me of the subject he had opened on our first visit, the one which had made the deepest impression. 'Have you,' I asked Houghton, 'anything by Chatterton?'

'I do indeed,' and he led me to a frail thing which the tormented boy had published in 1777: '*Poems*, supposed to have been written at Bristol, by Thomas Rowley, and others, in the Fifteenth Century, slightly foxed.' Newton had had only a forgery of the forgery, and it did not belong to him; Houghton had the forgery itself. Once more I was driven to speculation on the tragic life of this young genius, and I recalled the weeks I had labored over my verse play *Chatterton*, judging that experience to have been one of the most rewarding, though abortive, in which I ever engaged.

It would be difficult to explain the emotions of a writer when he stands in the presence of those great writers who have gone before and holds in his hands manuscripts over which they toiled or first editions of their books in which they wrote on publication day a dedication to some friend. At such times the unbroken heritage of a language becomes living and real, but even so, my experience in the big room at Houghton's library was eclipsed when at the close of my visit he led me to the smaller room to the left, for here he had a staggering collection of materials and editions relating to Lewis Carroll's *Alice's Adventures in Wonderland*, an entire room dedicated to one book, and the richness was quite overwhelming.

I asked Houghton how he had happened to concentrate on such an unlikely book, and he replied: 'It's one of the great flights of fancy. It captivates.'

Like the Newton collection, the Houghton books and manuscripts were dispersed at public auction, the difference being that Houghton disposed of his while very much alive; each man felt that continued circulation of his treasures through fresh hands would serve a good purpose. (Houghton could not bring himself to sell the *Alice's Adventures in Wonderland* materials; he gave them in toto to the Pierpont Morgan Library in New York.) These vanished libraries live on in memory, because each had been placed at my disposal at a time when I needed to be reminded of what a splendid contribution to life a book can be.

If one characteristic has marked my years as a writer it has been the careful attention I have paid to the making of a good book. I want it to look inviting, its maps to be accurate and pleasing, its type to be readable, its appearance to be within the great tradition. I seek to have it a companion with which the reader will associate for some weeks, and I want it to be remembered with affection as a pleasurable, rewarding experience. I do not write novels, or essays, or nonfiction; I write books, and the most successful one I have ever written is a small volume in tribute to the Japanese wood block artist, Katsushika Hokusai's *Manga*, in which old-style Japanese paper was used, folded in the ancient way and printed in part from wood blocks cut in the old manner. A. Edward Newton and his sublime forger Thomas J. Wise would have been proud of that book, as I am, for the making of a good book is a commendable act.

Three

When it came to painting, I was less fortunate in my youthful initiation to the arts. All started well with an introduction to the people caring for the amazing John G. Johnson Collection housed in a decaying mansion on Broad Street in Philadelphia. Mr. Johnson had been the epitome of the canny Philadelphia lawyer and as such had often traveled to England to supervise the purchase of those massive stately canvases by Gainsborough, Lawrence, Reynolds and Raeburn which newly-rich Philadelphia tycoons liked to buy. When these purchases were completed, Lawyer Johnson, on his own, used to trot off to Italy, where for himself he quietly purchased smaller canvases by artists like Botticelli, Crivelli, Cima and members of the underappreciated Sienese school. Of course, he stopped in Amsterdam, too, to acquire those glowing canvases by Steen, Ruysdael, Potter, Wouwerman and Rembrandt.

In time, families like the Wideners had rooms full of stuffy English portraits declining in reputation and value year by year, while Lawyer Johnson's mansion was crammed to overflowing with paintings which were going to become world famous with the passing years. I met Bernard Berenson when he was vetting the Johnson Italian paintings, and I watched as a great Dutch art historian did the same for the paintings of his countrymen.

The Johnson Collection was almost a perfect museum in which a young man could hone his artistic judgment because the paintings were thrown about helter-skelter— sometimes one fine Crivelli at the bottom, a Botticelli in the middle and a Sienese masterpiece at the top—so that by looking at one wall you could see some three dozen paintings with no blazing sign on any one proclaiming it to be as great as it was. You simply sat there and decided for yourself what was good and what not. I remember when I saw my first Canaletto and Guardi, one atop the other, and decided: 'This fellow Guardi is much the better,' a judgment I never surrendered.

My two score visits to the Johnson whetted my appetite for good painting, especially that by the so-called minor figures, and it was in this mood that I learned of the notorious collection of modern art assembled not far from Swarthmore: 'Jim, it's the greatest, believe me. This man has one of every major painter of the last fifty years.'

'Let's go see it,' I said enthusiastically.

'Unfortunately, no one can see it. He keeps it locked up. Especially from people in any way connected with a college.'

My informant was accurate in everything he had said about this stupendous collection on our doorstep, and the more I learned the more determined I became to break through the walls, the locks and the watchdogs to the collection of this modern Maecenas. So I began to lay plots.

Albert C. Barnes was an irascible genius

who had invented the miracle medicine Argy-rol, a fusion of silver nitrate and certain pro-teins, which, if placed in the eyes of newborn children, forestalls infections which once caused blindness and lesser afflictions. The invention made Barnes a multi-millionaire, but protracted court cases initiated by jeal-ous associates who claimed that they and not Barnes had done the discovering so embit-tered the man that he became reclusive.

When he started, with daring and deep appreciation, to buy non-classical paint-ings by little-known French painters like Cézanne, Renoir, Monet and Manet, citizens in the Philadelphia area, trained to like the big portraits of the Wideners, laughed at Barnes' pretensions, and certain college pro-fessors assured the public that the paintings Barnes was collecting were mostly junk. Un-derstandably, he became infuriated with all academics. He also became infuriated with a traffic light newly installed at a highway crossing he frequented; refusing to obey it or attend to the police summons which en-sued, he ploughed through one day and was wiped out by a huge truck which had the green light.

He despised with peculiar fury the art faculty at Bryn Mawr College, the art experts at the Philadelphia Museum and anyone associated with Swarthmore. With an acid pen he launched warfare against them all, vilifying anyone who thought he knew anything about art and attacking him with the most vituperative correspondence, public and private.

By his abominable manners he made himself a cause célèbre along the eastern seashore, and nothing pleased him better than to insult with the most shocking attacks anyone who presumed to seek entrance to his collection of paintings, which by now was world famous. Scholars, young students, curators, noted travelers—all were rejected scornfully, so there was no chance that I, with a Swarthmore affiliation, could gain entrance. I tried twice and was bitterly thrown back.

But the more I was rejected, the more determined I became to get in, because from time to time newspapers would carry accounts of the great treasures hidden away in Merion, and since I was now growing familiar with names like Cézanne and Renoir I lusted to see Barnes' examples, which were reported to be among the best in the world.

I am still proud of the stratagem I adopted to gain entrance; using a scrap of paper, I wrote in cramped longhand that I was a miner in the Pittsburgh area and that I kept on my wall a photograph of one of the fine pictures said to be in Mr. Barnes' collection, and each night when I came out of the mine I looked at it and promised myself that some day I would see that picture, and I wondered if I hitchhiked to Philadelphia, could I please see it?

I sent the letter to a college friend of mine who lived in the Pittsburgh area, Bill McLain who had gone to swank Kiskiminetas School, and he mailed it for me. Posthaste I received, through my Pittsburgh drop, an invitation from Barnes to come see him as soon as I could get east, and after a decent lapse I presented myself at Merion dressed in a miner's best suit.

It became one of the great days of my life! Barnes was not only gracious; he gave me a delightful meal, and then he took me into his gallery where a special light played on a Manet, beside which stood a Victrola on whose turntable he placed a record, which offered symphonic music while he explained the virtues of the painting and related its artistic forms to the music being played.

Alas, I cannot now remember what the painting was; it could even have been a Monet; but I can recall each movement of the music. It was Brahms' *First Symphony* and as the grand, sweeping surge of tone in the last movement filled the room it imbedded itself so deeply in my consciousness that it remains to this day one of my favorite passages in all of music.

I was ill-prepared for the glories of the Barnes Collection; I recall a stupefying assembly of paintings quite alien to the old masters of the Johnson Collection with which I was now so familiar. Cézanne quite escaped me; it was obvious that he couldn't draw. Renoir had certain moments of excellent color, but that was about all. Monet and Manet I could not differentiate, and I was relieved when he showed me his Italian masterpieces; later I would learn that these were mostly junk, whereas the French impressionists were even better than I had been told.

Following the Manet-Brahms affair, Barnes took me to another part of his museum where he had on an easel a Cézanne landscape beside which stood a series of hand-carved wooden implements used by the Pennsylvania Dutch, plus a different Victrola. This time he played Beethoven's *Seventh* as he explained that the three art forms—Cézanne, Beethoven, the German woodcarver—were really all one artistic impulse. Now I caught what he was endeavoring to say: 'Joy! The joy of good workmanship! It doesn't really matter how you express it!' He spoke with exclamation points, growling, no neck, excitable hands, red of face, and always returning to his basic principle: 'All art is one! But with the shit they throw at you in the museums they do their best to hide that fact. Never go near public museums, young man! They'll ruin you!'

We spent a long day together, one of the best I would ever have, for although I could not follow all of Barnes' reasonings nor appreciate his more daring canvases, I had no doubt whatever that I had been in touch with an original human being who responded passionately to whatever he was doing.

I caught my first taste of that passion when word circulated in Philadelphia's art circles that 'this clever kid out at Swarthmore outfoxed the old bearcat. Not only wormed his way into the museum but had a five hour lecture from Barnes himself.' Of course rumors of the escapade reached Barnes, who sent operatives over to our campus to look into the matter and more particularly into my background.

Then began a battle which never relaxed until the day he was ground down by the truck. Wherever I went his henchmen followed me, causing minor troubles. He wrote to me often, reminding me of the condign punishment that awaited me when he got around to it. When I became a writer he fastened onto me like a leech, tormenting, challenging, abusing and in general making himself a public nuisance. I don't know how he kept track of me, but in those difficult days when I earned little from my pen I had to depend on public lecturing upon literature, and often when I started my lecture I

photograph © 1993 by The Barnes Foundation

Albert C. Barnes with his dog in front of
Matisse's *Red Madras Headdress*

would see, sitting balefully in the front row, red-faced Albert C. Barnes, waiting malevolently until the question-and-answer period, when he would rip into me with some erudite query that I had no chance of answering.

Once I was invited to give a major address at the University of Pennsylvania, and apparently this conjunction of two institutions he despised—Penn and Michener—was too inviting to be passed over, so he sent me a long letter threatening to dissect me publicly if I dared to step on the Penn stage. In one of the most deplorable errors of my life I thought I was clever enough to meet his threats with some of my own and sent him a sharp reply, which at the time I considered a rather clever bit of literary repartee.

What a horrible miscalculation. Barnes photographed my letter plus three of his own, added a terrifying covering letter and shipped the whole off to the Penn faculty, who met me at my hotel two hours before the proposed lecture. They were sweating, and by the time I finished reading Barnes' threats against Penn, the Penn faculty, the

City of Philadelphia, and most particularly me, I was sweating, too, rather heavily.

It was a gruesome evening, because Barnes had filled the first row with henchmen from his museum, still closed to the public, and these men and women glared at me through the introduction, obviously prepared to tear me apart as soon as I began speaking. More perspiration, but to my surprise they allowed me to speak without interruptions; however, when time came for questions from the floor no one was able to speak but they. With savage thrusts they assaulted every major point I had been trying to make, and then Barnes himself rose, chin thrust out, voice rumbling: 'It must be quite obvious to the public here that you know nothing about your subject. To the reporters present I issue this challenge. I will debate this man Michener in the public press, on this platform, on radio, anywhere, any time. And I will prove to the world what a fraud he is.'

The media, sensing the start of a public brawl which could be fueled for years, pestered me to accept the challenge, but I had had enough, because what the reporters could not know was that Barnes had started sending me a chain of the wildest, most profane and vicious letters imaginable, assaulting me on every possible count. In fact, they were so scurrilous that he had learned from previous similar barrages against the colleges and museums that he must not send them through the mail for fear of imprisonment. Instead, he sent them to my home some fifty miles away by chauffeured messenger, who always delivered them with a smug smile which I found more infuriating than the letters.

It was apparent that Barnes had developed a monomaniacal hatred against which I would prove quite powerless, especially since he was prepared to spend full time on his avocation while I had to earn a living. It was a most unfair confrontation; he was more clever than I, more vicious, more witty, and far wealthier. As gracefully as I could, which was not very, I withdrew from a battle which I had started by invading the Barnes Castle under false pretenses and which for a short while I had falsely assumed I could continue.

Three aspects of the fray abide in my

memory. Once when Barnes had followed me to Allentown, to give me a true lambasting in the question period, he came up after the display, threw his heavy arm around my shoulder and said gleefully: 'I really gave you hell tonight, didn't I?' He was a much older man than I, but I used the familiar: 'Barnes, you'll live to see the day when you beg me to come visit your lousy museum.' Clapping me on the shoulder strongly enough to make me stagger he said: 'That'll be the day after hell freezes over,' and I told him: 'The temperature just dropped twenty degrees.'

Later he devised a diabolical scheme to destroy me, one so fiendish that I still chuckle over it with delight. To my home he sent a rather wispy man who made this astonishing proposal: 'My mother works for the Barnes Museum as a charlady and she knows that you want to see the paintings again, so she makes this suggestion. You come to our house in Merion and we'll dress you in charlady's costume and she'll take you into the museum as her assistant. You'll carry a bucket and stay close to her, and you can see the whole place. How about it?'

The plot, straight out of Falstaff, with newspaper photographers prepared for the great unveiling, was so transparent that I wondered how Barnes could have conceived it, but to give him pleasure I went along and said: 'Now that's a damned clever idea.' I said I'd come to Merion for the penetration, but when Barnes' henchman called in the morning to be sure I'd be there to dress in my charwoman's costume I told him: 'You tell your boss I read the Falstaff plays fifteen years ago.' I heard no more about that caper.

Some years after Barnes had died I had my last confrontation with him. Art lovers throughout Pennsylvania objected and quite properly, to the fact that the Barnes Foundation which now owned the paintings and ran the museum enjoyed tax-exempt status from the public while refusing, in accordance with Barnes' ill-tempered will, to allow any of the public to see the paintings. The Barnes people argued that the museum was actually a school and that to allow public access would amount to disrupting school procedures.

The Commonwealth of Pennsylvania brought suit to force the opening of the museum to the general public, and in the process of the trial government lawyers insisted that I testify to the malpractices of Barnes during his lifetime and after his death via his restrictive will. This I refused to do on the grounds that while alive Barnes had more than bested me in debate and to strike at him now that he was dead and incapable of self-defense would be craven. The lawyers were disgusted, for they believed that for the first time they had a chance to break this improper will; they felt that every decent citizen ought to rise up and help strike it down. To tell the truth, I feared that if I did speak out, it would be Barnes who would rise from the grave to strike me down, and I could visualize him throwing that big hand over my shoulder when the deed was done and saying: 'Boy, Michener, we gave them hell tonight, didn't we?'

Four

It was with memories like this that I flew, some time ago, to Hawaii to do research on the South Pacific, and like many another traveler I discovered on the third day that I had run out of reading material, so I walked down to the Waikiki branch of Woolworth's on Kalakaua Avenue, just off Lewers Avenue and the sixth-floor apartment in which I had written *Hawaii*. In those far-off days our apartment had been the topmost in Waikiki; now I could scarcely find it among the new skyscrapers.

I remembered that Woolworth's (having learned that tourists like me often ran out of reading material), always had a large stock of paperbacks, and I intended to catch up on several authors about whom I was inadequately informed: Robert Coover, Thomas Berger, Joan Didion, Anne Rice, John Irving, and I looked forward to some days of good reading.

The Waikiki Woolworth's has one of the most unusual book departments in Christendom. Along a dark wall more than a hundred feet long and with an aisle not more than three feet wide the store offers a complete wall covered with nothing but paperbacks, thousands of them really, but even a casual inspection satisfies the would-be reader that Coover, Berger and Didion are not favorites; vast displays of gothics, romances, westerns and mysteries are the predilected fare. But I had learned long ago that if one searched diligently one could find an occasional Cheever, Updike or Malamud which had slipped in. I was somewhat depressed to find that only one of my books, *Hawaii*, was available, and none of the good books by other writers.

In disappointment I was about to leave the store when my eye chanced to fall upon a display of some fifty books, all with the same 1870s Valentine's Day cover, a lacy boudoir type of thing, identical over the fifty books, each of which proclaimed that it was 'a novel of enduring romance' by that queen of storytellers GRACE LIVINGSTON HILL. On the reverse side of each book appeared the same paragraph, painstakingly crafted by experts for salesmanship, every word having been honed to perfection. No better summary of Mrs. Hill's genius could have been constructed:

> The beloved author of over 100 books read and cherished by millions, Mrs. Hill creates thrilling stories of inspiring, wholesome people whose ardent faith and overflowing hearts cope triumphantly with the problems of the modern world.

I knew immediately that I must purchase from this amazing display of valentines, and at first I selected one which broke new ground, so far as I was concerned, for it was a western, and I had not previously known that Mrs. Hill had used such a milieu: *The Man of the Desert*. A young woman finds

new faith and lasting love with the missionary who saves her life.' It was #63 in the
current series, but when I looked at the
copyright page I was disappointed to find
that it had been published in 1914 by Flem-
ing Revell, and I did not care to read a non-
Lippincott book.

I chose instead #40, '*The Tryst*. A troubled
girl and a dedicated young minister grow
together in their love of God ... and each
other. Lippincott, 1921.' It was a charming
story in which ardent looks and fingertips
romantically touching were a nice relief
from the brazen young women who were
then parading Kalakaua Avenue in bikinis
and gulping ice-cream sundaes in Woolworth's while dressed in halter tops and not
much else.

As I stood with my purchase at the check-
out counter I reflected that whereas
A. Edward Newton was dead, with the
books he had written consigned to limbo,
and whereas Albert C. Barnes was also dead
in that fearful crash, with his essays on art
long forgotten and his will broken by the
Commonwealth, so that even now I could
enter his museum and inspect at leisure his

marvelous Cézannes, his often tedious Renoirs, and his laughable classics, Grace Livingston Hill was still alive with her books covering an entire wall in Honolulu: sixty-four titles so far re-published, and more than forty still to come. It was a triumph, I thought, of honest sentiment over pedantry, and while I waited for the sales girl to get to me I visualized those three Philadelphians who had been so important to me when I was a college student trying to form judgments on art.

There was Mrs. Hill, as gracious a lady as her time produced, quiet, self-effacing, grand in the old-fashioned sense, dashing off her two books a year, decade after decade, and holding her faithful audience even two score years after her death . . . increasing it substantially, for as I move about the country I stop frequently at bookstores to check how the Hill books are doing, and I was told only this morning at a small store in my home town: 'We have only eighteen different titles on hand now. Very difficult to keep all sixty-four in stock, they go out so fast.'

There was A. Edward Newton as I remembered him in the colored frontispiece to his 1933 volume *End Papers*, a chunky little Pickwick dressed in the 1790 red hunting costume of his beloved Jorrocks, whose first editions he had in great number. Newton titled his portrait 'The Book-Collector Masquerading as Master of Hounds.' The protruding upper lip is firm, the eyes as quizzical as ever, and I can see him standing before his rows of books, speaking of Surtees and Dickens, whom he worshipped, but always of Dr. Johnson and Blake, who had dominated his life for so long. Newton was a funny, opinionated, dear fellow who communicated his love of books to everyone, and now he and his books were gone.

And there was Albert C. Barnes who had used his art as a weapon to destroy others. When I appeared before him as a coal miner he had been so warmhearted and outgoing that I still remembered him glowing as the Brahms *First* unfolded; I could still feel the excitement in his arm as he hugged me and whispered: 'I really gave you hell tonight, didn't I?' What a vivid man he was, how his feuds echoed up and down the Schuylkill when he was at his venomous best. He

An imaginary portrait by H.J. Brothers

A. Edward Newton

taught me who Cézanne was, and he had some of the best works that supreme master ever painted.

How lucky I was to have known at a formative stage in my life three such vigorous people: Newton was convinced that Dr. Johnson, Blake and Keats were among the immortals and said so, with their works in his hands to prove it; Barnes knew that his painters were on their way to Parnassus; and Mrs. Hill knew that her novels were at least as good as Jane Austen's and probably better than Emily Brontë's, for in her writing the latter did parade some of the uglier aspects of feminine nature.

When I reached home I looked into the matter of her continued success, for even today she sells far more copies per year of her works than Jane Austen and Emily Brontë combined. Bantam Books reprints in paperback some sixty of her books, recostuming them every three or four years in bright new covers; when I went to my booksellers yesterday to see what was available I found the lacy valentine covers had been replaced by extremely handsome new ones lettered in a more austere modern style as if the books had been written last year.

I asked a competitor about the Hill phenomenon and he explained: 'In the gothic and romance fields the whole problem is to have enough books to establish a series. Then you can command shelf space, exhibition space. For example, our company has some great individual titles, but no series, so we get killed in the marketplace. But we've just entered into a contract with a manuscript-providing service which will ensure us four books a month, which we'll sell almost like magazines. Two each month will be laid in the moors of eighteenth-century England, with maybe an occasional excursion into Scotland. The third will be a mansion on the Hudson. And the fourth alternates between a castle on the Rhine and a chateau on the Loire. We have great hopes for such a series, and with good reason.

'The genius of the Bantam people was that someone in their office remembered the Grace Livingston Hill books, more than a hundred of them, and with one swell foop as we say they bought the rights and were in business. A hundred titles, great subject matter, and all the shelf space they can use. Overnight they found themselves at the head of the line.'

When I sought to confirm these facts with Bantam Books they told me:

I checked with our executive editor Grace Bechtold about how we happened upon the Grace Livingston Hill books. As she remembers, one of our southern sales representatives called her to our attention. The rest, as they say, is history.

We began publishing her books in 1967 and have a total imprint figure of 23,942,000 copies for 64 titles. At present we keep 16 titles in print and have a reissue program of one per month. Although the books are not selling quite as well as they once did, there is still a remarkably strong, steady demand.

On inquiry I also found that Amereon Limited, a house in Mattituck, New York, which does hard-cover reprints of the classics, offers sixty-eight of Mrs. Hill's titles at a typical price of $15.95 each.

Now, as I recall those two visits with her I find myself reflecting that fifty years hence my books, like A. Edward Newton's, could well be gathering dust while hers, decked out in new covers which would reflect the tastes of the twenty-first century, will be covering whole walls in Honolulu, Seattle and San Antonio, because as the exquisitely phrased editor's statement says: 'She creates thrilling stories of inspiring wholesome people whose ardent faith and overflowing hearts cope triumphantly with the problems of the modern world.' And one can be confident that these valiant, religious souls will cope just as well in 2014 as they did in 1914.

TESTIMONY

— ◇ —

Originally published in a limited edition of 200 copies by a close personal friend of James A. Michener, A. Grove Day of White Knight Press in Honolulu, Hawaii in 1983.

Rondeau

Of a Writer on Attaining Age Seventy-five

I owe the world a debt of grace,
Some rental on the precious space
I am allowed to occupy,
From whence I publish forth my cry
That magnifies the human race.

I never sought fame's harsh embrace.
I could depart without a trace.
The world owes me no laurels high . . .
    I owe the world.

So I would deem it no disgrace
Should fate determine to erase

All I have done and nullify
My passioned books, letting them die.
The world owes me no special place . . .
  I owe the world.

photo courtesy of James A. Michener

James A. Michener writing *Tales of the
South Pacific*

Credo

In writing numerous books, I have been obligated to study the problem of effective narration and have evolved a set of beliefs which govern my work:

... I must never forget that I am a part of the animal kingdom. This governing principle is not original with me, for it was voiced beautifully in the Bible, *Ecclesiastes* 3:18-19: 'Concerning the estate of the sons of men, God might manifest them that they might see that they themselves are beasts. For that which befalleth the sons of men befalleth beasts; even one thing befalleth them: as the one dieth, so dieth the other; yea, they all have one breath, so that a man hath no preeminence above a beast: for all is vanity.'

. . . Like the other animals, I inhabit a finite earth that is worth knowing and preserving.

. . . But I also live in an infinite universe that never can be fully known.

. . . I share the earth with other human animals like myself, whose behavior and systems merit study and analysis.

. . . In seeking evidence, I must rely on nothing at second hand.

. . . In devising a novel, it is perilous to start from an exciting theme. In general, a novel *about something* is always a disaster.

. . . An effective novel starts with characters, grows with them, and matures intellectually and spiritually with them. But they must be seen in their setting, engaged by the great themes of their time.

. . . The greatest novels are written without any recourse to research other than the writer's solitary inspection of the human experience. Flaubert, Dostoyevski, Jane Austen, Turgenev and Henry James exemplify this truth.

. . . Novels, of course, can be based on research, but artistically they must always remain in a secondary category. Zola, Balzac, Tolstoy, Dickens and Dreiser come to mind; but if one could equal the best novels of these men, he would be more than satisfied.

. . . To praise a writer for having done research is like praising a bus driver for knowing how to shift gears; if he can't perform that simple function, he has no right to climb into the bus.

. . . What research is done should be on the iceberg principle: one-tenth visible in the finished work, nine-tenths submerged, but available to give the whole stability and a sense of force.

. . . I have always thought of myself as a freak, off to one side, who had the great good fortune to stumble into precisely the style of writing for which my personality and education fitted me. Lucky is the artist to whom that happens.

. . . In planning a novel, I accomplish little before the architecture is settled.

. . . In choosing words for a novel, music is everything.

. . . In acquiring a verbal style, establish a

balance between English words of Latin or Greek derivation and those of Saxon.

. . . In acquiring a narrative style, establish a balance between two types of writing: scene (in which characters talk and act) and carry (in which they are talked about and acted upon). To write either type well is difficult; to alternate and link them artistically is the soul of narration.

. . . The artistic linkage of elements is a major factor in compelling narrative. 'Meanwhile, back at the ranch' became a classic; alas, its triteness now condemns it, but the writer must invent his own attractive alternatives.

. . . In attracting the attention of the reader, the sovereign device is to deal with a notable theme; in holding his attention, the sovereign technique is verisimilitude.

. . . Make the opening chapters of a novel difficult, so as to discourage certain readers. (There are some who ought not to waste their time on what I have written; there are others on whom I do not wish to waste my time.)

. . . Heavy symbolism and strained metaphor are for writers who are geniuses or who attend courses in creative writing.

... Using arcane, amusing dialect is a temptation to be avoided; books which rely on this often enjoy brief notoriety and long eclipse.

... Write always for one's self, for if a book is of compelling interest to me, it stands a chance of being so to others.

... If a manuscript is worthy of publication, it has a right to appear in a book-form which is attractive, maintains the great traditions, and is inviting to the reader. Physically a book should be a thing of joy.

... Writing is a profession demanding enormous skill and should be rewarded commensurately. Dr. Johnson knowingly overstated the case when he growled: 'No man but a blockhead ever wrote, except for money.' But in order to protect myself from corruption, I ought to give most of what I earn to causes harmonious to my personal aspirations.

... I am not an author. I am a writer.

... Above all, a writer must bear testimony. His work should present a consistent, constructive whole.

Rondeau

Of a Compulsive Worker on His Eightieth Birthday

Full eighty times the cock has crowed
Not for the day but for the year,
Shouting his admonition clear:
'Awake! The testing time is near
And you must reap the crop you
      sowed.'

Each dawn I left my warm abode
And worked till every sheaf was stowed,
Then checked to see the field was clear
   Full eighty times.

And as I sweated by the road,
Apologetic for the code
That drove me so, I chanced to hear
God's voice: 'I shall not interfere,
But you toil in a field I hoed
   Full eighty times.'

photo by George Holmes,
Archer M. Huntington Art Gallery

A Faithful Remembrance

Older writers are often asked which novels, read when young, influenced them. But since the answer must usually be delivered on the spot and under pressure, a good deal of posing and false recollection results. Now, in sober reflection, I would like to name those books which did actually determine my attitude toward the novel, my style of writing, and my general interpretation of life.

We were an extremely poor family, but each night my hardworking mother assembled the orphan children she took into her home and read to them from the great novelists. So before I could recite the alphabet,

I was familiar with Dickens, Thackeray, Reade and Sienkiewicz. Of these wonderful books, one stands preeminent, *Great Expectations*. It started everything, and I am always pleased when I hear some respectable critic say that he or she considered it a masterpiece. It reminds me that I began at the top.

The first book I read on my own was also a masterpiece, in its way: *Tom Swift and His Electric Rifle*. The heroes were heroic, and the villains dastardly, a tradition which operated with great success in novels like *The Virginian* and *The Count of Monte Cristo* and in plays like *Othello* and *Siegfried*.

A sleazy salesman conned my Aunt Laura into buying a complete set of Balzac's works; she could ill afford such a purchase, but to me it was worth a million dollars because the first really fine book I read, at the age of twelve or thirteen, was *Pere Goriot*, and it launched my intellectual life. I read almost all of Balzac and revere him as my prime mentor.

I came to poetry late, but I absorbed it avidly, always preferring Keats to Shelley, Wordsworth to Byron, Arnold to Coleridge, and Milton to Spenser. Shakespeare stood on a mountain peak, and Chaucer perplexed me. I memorized great slabs of poetry—glowing passages of *Othello*, *The Eve of Saint Agnes*, *Elegy Wrote in a Country Churchyard*, *Lycidas* and the *Rubaiyat*. I knew by heart several dozen sonnets and a score of the short lyrics, which I loved. I could never have become a writer without this flow of magnificent words—not ideas, words—cascading through my mind, and I still read aloud every sentence I try to write, endeavoring to catch that easy, steady flow of Gray or Keats.

It will be noted, of course, that I am inclined toward the didactic, preferring poems like Wordsworth's *Intimations of Immortality* and Milton's *On His Blindness*. Mine was a heavy touch rather than a light, glancing one.

In college, to which I reported well prepared in much of the foregoing, I studied most of the traditional novels and read widely in those not assigned. I was selective in what I took to my bosom, and Richardson, Fielding, Sterne and Smollett I passed by; I was not ready for them. I did the same with *Return of the Native*, but *Tess of the D'Urbervilles* stunned me with its passion, its compelling characters, and its great sweep of tragedy. It still seems a remarkable achievement, but the Hardy novel I recommend to young writers is *The Mayor of Casterbridge*, whose opening chapter is one of the world's finest examples of how to start a narrative; it is both compelling and premonitory.

On my own I discovered the book which first gave me a strong sense of how a novel was constructed—Arnold Bennett's *The Old Wives' Tale*, which seemed so extraordinary in its quiet use of everyday material that I read it several times to see just how its effects were achieved. My attitude toward narration was profoundly influenced by this straightforward, no-nonsense tale.

The acerbic character of many good novels was first exemplified for me by a book not widely read today but one which still constituted something of a scandal in the 1930s, and it echoes in memory for a bizarre reason. We students were required by Professor Robert Spiller, a great teacher and a fine historian of American literature, to give a fifteen-minute review of a major novel, and I was assigned *The Way of All Flesh* but had not the time actually to read it. Instead I ducked out to a theater where the motion picture was playing with Emil Jannings in the lead. I must say in all honesty that I thought the story rather inflated and could not understand why it was considered a classic, but if that was the case, so be it.

In class next day I rose, stated that I had read and enjoyed *The Way of All Flesh*, whereupon I gave a rather animated summary of the story:

The hero is an honest, hardworking German small businessman in Wisconsin. He is married, but unfortunately he falls in love with a woman of loose morals. To finance his fast living with her he steals a large sum of money, runs away to Chicago, and we watch him as he sinks lower and lower into the morass of the great city.

The novel ends dramatically with the hero returning to his home town on

Christmas Eve, during a blizzard, and we see him crawl through the storm, to his old home where his family has reestablished itself.

Through the storm he peers through the window at the warm, Christmas-tree happiness of the family he had lost. Brave and responsible at last, he goes off into the storm without revealing his identity to them.

Dr. Spiller sat spellbound as I thus summarized one of the strongest English novels, but two students who had also elected to report on it began to giggle, and I could hear whispers passing through the classroom, so that my peroration, in which I referred to the high moral values of the novel, was engulfed with laughter.

All Dr. Spiller said was: 'You have given such a stirring review of Emil Jannings' movie, why don't you come back on Monday and review Ernest Pontifex's novel?' When I read it, I understood why it was considered so powerful, with its sharp comments on clerical life in rural England, and I could say later, with strict accuracy: 'The book was better than the movie.'

In college I also made my acquaintance with what I believe to be the most completely satisfying novel ever constructed, Flaubert's *Madame Bovary*. I did not appreciate it fully on first reading, but during summer vacation, when I read it again, I saw with what skill the characters were drawn, their setting established and the plot woven about them until they were entangled in tragedy. The beginner who meets Emma Bovary early is fortunate indeed. I was also enchanted by Mrs. Gaskell's *Cranford*, a lesser book I still read periodically, and by *Wuthering Heights*. Jane Austen, Charlotte Brontë and Walter Scott I missed, and I tried to read Conrad but at that time could make nothing of him. Later, when I knew the Pacific he had sailed and the islands he had frequented, I concluded that *Victory* was the best short novel I had so far read, and it still excels *Ethan Frome* and *The Old Man and the Sea*.

I ended my first two years of college with extremely wide knowledge of the novel but without any personal attitude toward fiction or narrative; I had been a consumer, never a potential producer. And then one summer, with ample space, I read *Vanity Fair*, and for the first time found myself absolutely enfolded by a book. I could see the characters, follow their misbehaviors, appreciate the settings in which they operated and view with dismay the closing pages of the book when I realized that I was about to leave them forever. That was when I discovered the basic magic of writing: that the novelist can create a little universe in which the reader lives for a given period and from which he departs with regret.

I jumped immediately to *Anna Karenina*, with the same results. I was transported to Russia, engulfed, bewildered and evermore a prisoner of the novel as a form. I now understood how the creative writer assembles and manipulates his cast, what old tricks he uses, what new devices he must invent for his particular story; and I believe it must have been that summer when I first suspected that perhaps I too might be able to invent and control those components.

I have watched with sadness, in recent years, as critics have launched harsh attacks on both *Vanity Fair* and *Anna Karenina*, and this has driven me to reread both novels to see if the re-evaluations are correct. Alas, in some respects they are. *Vanity Fair* is coy in spots and sometimes ill paced. *Anna Karenina* has that intolerably long and heavy postlude following the death of Anna. But when I was twenty and needed something like these two novels to awaken my eyes, they were marvelous, fashioned especially for me, and I would have been impoverished had they not been at hand. The would-be writer is fortunate when he finds the right novel at the right moment for the illumination of his mind, and most unfortunate if the telling novel is not available.

In the two years after college, still without a style of my own, I had the good luck to teach in a private school where I was required to be in my room six nights a week from seven to eleven, and I spent these nights reading European literature. After that I traveled in Europe for two years and continued the same reading program. Next I spent three years in another school where I likewise had a heavy schedule of study hall and dormitory surveillance, which meant that at the end of this seven-year stretch I had actually read almost every fine European novel that had been translated into English.

I have never been able to explain this curious development. Why the European novel? Why start with the French novel at age twelve, then specialize in the English novel during college, and leapfrog cleanly over the American novel, turning to the European in post-college days? I cannot even guess how this happened, except that good colleges in my day tended to specialize in English history, European thought, and English literature. Regarding American literature I was almost stupid.

But I gave myself a course in the European novel that was incomparable: Undset, Hamsun, Galdós, Reymont, Couperus, Nexø, Goncharov, Montherlant, Gorky, Gide, Svevo, Dostoyevski, Tolstoy, Lagerlof, Prus, Stendhal and Cervantes. From Asia I read with the keenest delight the superlative novel of ancient Japan, *Genji*, and the even more powerful novel of ancient China, published in English under the title *Robbers and Soldiers*, but I found them more exotic than instructive. I was not mature enough in those years to appreciate Proust, Joyce and Kafka, but of course I doubled back later to study them intensively; however, they never exerted the influence on me they should have and I still feel the loss. Because I was overseas at a critical stage of my reading, I also missed the American writers Fitzgerald, Wolfe and Faulkner; I knew them, of course, knew them well, but not in that first fiery frenzy when opinions and standards are built.

At the conclusion of this intensive self-education, I knew most of what there was to be known about the novels of the world, insofar as the consumer was concerned, and very little where the producer was involved. At about this time I was required, at Harvard, to take the Graduate Record Examination, a test for all young men and women in the better universities who sought advanced degrees; it was an excellent test, requiring five afternoons, as I recall, and covering six or eight major fields of learning. In 'Literature' I received a mark so high that it stood not only at the head of many thousands but also off the top of the page by about four inches. I knew what the novel was but not how it was created.

Acknowledging my partial education, I cast about for some essay which would instruct me in the mysteries, and after wasting my time on various books purporting to explain how to write a novel, I stumbled by the greatest blind luck upon that little book which has instructed hundreds of serious writers and which is revered in many countries of the world by those who know it well. During one of the World Wars, a German scholar named Auerbach found himself immured in Constantinople. Without many books, he was thrown back upon his own resources, so he began to reflect on what narrative (mimesis or imitation) consisted of, and starting with the simplest of man's recountings he moved to Homer, to the Bible, to the great storytellers, and finally to the most advanced and complex narrators of our day, including Virginia Woolf, for whom he had great regard. When I finished with *Mimesis* I knew what narrative was, and if I were working with a group of young people who seriously desired to become writers I would ask them to read only this book. I have met various experts in different countries who have said the same.

Now that I knew what a novel was, it became imperative that I uncover what capacities I myself might have, and four novels fell to hand—no one as great as those mentioned hitherto, but each of superlative importance to me because it found me at the precise moment when I needed it. Just as *Anna Karenina* and *Vanity Fair*, by no means the greatest novels in the world, awakened me to what the novel could be because I was at that moment prepared to listen, so now these four magnificent cicerones appeared to give instruction.

The most important novel I was ever to read was a little-known work by a Dutch writer who had lived in Java and who wrote under the nom-de-plume of Multatuli (Many Sorrows). Appalled by how what should have been an island paradise was being corrupted, he wrote a curious novel called *Max Havelaar*, which in many ways was the traditional novel of colonial protest; it could have been written in any Central American country had some young American with talent simply looked at the banana trade. Its importance to me lay in the fact that E. Douwes Dekker, Multatuli's real name, wrote with passion and crammed into his novel literally anything that came to mind; it was a terrible hodge-podge really, with lists and accounts and animadversions, but in the end added up to the greatest novel yet written in Dutch, and some years ago formed the basis for a stunning motion picture, the best ever made in Holland. It was, in short, an authentic masterpiece, and I knew this the moment I began to read it. What did it do for me? It showed me that a novel is whatever a burning imagination says it is. What does a novel contain? Any damned thing a talented writer proposes to put in it. What does a novel strive for? A blow to the heart. If I had never read *Max Havelaar*, I might still have become a writer, but never the kind of writer I became.

This wonderful Dutch novel was raw and lacking in suavity, and I knew it, but my next two introductions fortunately corrected that imbalance. Aldous Huxley's *Point Counter Point* gave me as much sheer pleasure as any book I ever read; it was a naughty, urbane, scintillating delight and showed me several things: how deft a cultured man could be in his use of words; how a narrative filled with many disparate types could be held together; how a complex account could be kept moving forward; and how sardonic comment on contemporary society could be utilized to produce quite marvellous results. It also taught me that never in a hundred years could I write a book half as good, in that genre, because I was a person totally contrary to Huxley. In other words, he showed me conclusively what I could not do.

For sheer reading pleasure, few books gave me more delight than Thomas Mann's *The Magic Mountain*, which had all the glitter of *Point Counter Point* plus a philosophical depth that Huxley never attained, and for some years I considered it the best twentieth-century novel I'd read; but it was a much different Mann novel which became truly important to me, for again it appeared before me at the moment when I needed the instruction that it could give. *Buddenbrooks* taught me how a family could be utilized as the hero of a novel, and in three impassioned readings I followed with amazement Mann's skill in holding his story together while retaining the full interest of his reader. It is obvious to me now that the rowdy power of *Max Havelaar* combined with the special elegance of *Buddenbrooks* formed my attitude toward and understanding of the long narrative novel. *The Magic Mountain* is by all accounts a much superior novel, but it could never do for me what *Buddenbrooks* did, and so it was the latter which served as my teacher.

It is curious that, at a time when I was so hungry for instruction in how to use a family as motive force, I did not discover *The Forsyte Saga*. I tried four or five times to get started in it, but could generate no interest whatever; perhaps I needed the heavier Germanic touch. In later years, however, I was like millions of other Americans captivated by the BBC television rendering of the Galsworthy novels and rushed into print with an essay extolling the series; but when belatedly I returned to the novels themselves I still found them tedious. I much preferred Trollope.

When I was about ready to try my own

hand at a novel, I had the great good fortune to read seriously an American novel
which I had failed to get into when it first
appeared. Up to this moment the best American novel I had read was Frank Norris'
McTeague, which had swept me off my feet
one summer when I stumbled upon it without warning, but I recognized it as rather
raw, and learned little from it except that a
book like it could be great fun.

Now I studied seriously Theodore Dreiser's *An American Tragedy* and was bowled
over by its massive weight, its stillful construction, its compelling story-telling and its
painful characterizations. I concluded then,
and still believe, that insofar as gravity is
concerned it is our greatest American novel,
ceding place to *Moby Dick* only if inspired
poetry and intensity of concept are held to
be preeminent characteristics. I find *Moby
Dick* to be a timeless, countryless work; I
find Dreiser's novel to be exactly what its title proclaims, a tragedy deeply rooted in
America, and I sorely needed such a book. I
revere it.

I now had in my mental equipment a theory of the novel, a concept of how free the

form could be, and an understanding of how the story of a family or group of families could be separated into strands and interwoven, but the characteristic which would mark most distinctly my own writing I did not yet have: I mean the firm placing of incident within its geographical setting past to present. This I obtained from an impassioned reading while serving on Guadalcanal in World War II of a little-known book which enchanted me, *The Timeless Land*, by the Australian writer Eleanor Dark. It was a spacious book in its probing of the aboriginal mind in its ancient setting, and it showed me what a writer could achieve with such material. I remain profoundly indebted to it.

That with all my reading of the world's great classics I should have settled upon *Max Havelaar* and *The Timeless Land* as my major preceptors teaches only one thing: that book which is significant to a forming mind will be the one which reaches that mind at the crucial moment when fructification is possible and needed. And that is why young people should read widely and not be overawed by the opinions of others. What critic in the world could have directed me to these two minor works which were to explode my mind, enabling it to reach its own potential?

There was one other book of considerable technical importance, but I shall not award it a marginal number because it also taught me only one thing: how to link narrative passages so that the story can leap from one setting to another, from one group of characters to another quite similar. *The Forty Days of Musa Dagh* is a brilliant example of artistic linkage, because Werfel, if he wishes to tell his story effectively, must jump back and forth between the besieging Turks and the besieged Armenians. I was impressed by the skill with which he managed these shifts while maintaining the reader's interest in both groups. Keats faced the same problem in his *The Eve of St. Agnes*:

So, purposing each moment to retire,
She lingered still. Meantime, across the
    moors,
Had come young Porphyro, with heart
    on fire . . .

'Meanwhile' is one of the most pregnant words of the English language and its proper use, or that of its logical substitutes, can enhance a narrative.

At long last, at the age of forty, when many writers have already retired, I felt that my apprenticeship was finished and I was ready to begin.

Today, when I am at work, three books are always at hand, and I consult them daily.

The World Almanac answers quickly and concisely the kind of question which so often confronts the writer: When the Siege of Vicksburg ended on 4 July 1863 what day of the week was it? (Saturday). What foreign country is about the same size as Texas? (Burma). Who was James K. Polk's vice president? (George M. Dallas).

Roget's Thesaurus would be an admirable tool were I bright enough to use it. I am not. Its massive construction, with thousands of words spilling over every pair of pages, is too complex for my simple mind. Like most professional writers I prefer a more easy-to-use dictionary type in which a single word is given in alphabetical order, followed by its many synonyms. *Rodale's The Synonym Finder* is unequalled for simplicity and wealth of entry. I use *Rodale* every day I work and have never found it giving me a totally new word; what it does so well is remind me of other old ones that I already know but cannot at the moment recall. For example, 'operose' is offered as a synonym for 'industrious,' and whereas Bill Buckley or John Updike might use it deftly, for me to do so would be wrong. But I am pleased to be reminded that 'sedulous' and 'pertinacious,' words that I might use, are available.

I have written perhaps as many words as most writers, but I remain awed by the wonder of the English language. I own numerous foreign-language dictionaries, big ones with supposedly full vocabularies, and they run to some 70,000 words for Spanish, 100,000 for German, and perhaps 120,000 for French. My big English dictionary contains 550,000, a consequence of two conditions: our language provides for every concept a word of Latin or Greek derivation, but also a Germanic one, so that it is really a double language; also, English has borrowed happily and shamelessly from almost every other language on earth. I am very fond of using an expressive Japanese word picked up in Korea; *honcho*, a noun meaning 'top dog' or 'big enchilada' or 'grand mahoof' or 'top banana,' or any of a dozen other epithets, but shorter and stronger than any of them. It can also be used a a verb, as in the plaintive cry we used to hear: 'Who in the hell is honchoing this deal?'

I love the richness, the complexity of English, and realize with awe that as I approach the end of a writing career I have not yet begun to master the language. I still don't understand how 'cleave' can have two completely opposite meanings, 'to cut into separate parts' and 'to stick fast.' I avoid the term. I refuse to believe that 'presently' means not 'now,' but 'sometime in the future.' But my major problem with the language I love is that I cannot master its spelling. I've written a lot about the military but do not know whether they dress in 'khaki,' 'kakhi,' or 'khakhi.' I cannot spell 'rhythm' without looking it up, because I know its sister word is 'rime,' but also 'rhyme.' I use 'fulfill' a lot, but never without suspicion. The rule that says that a consonant must be doubled when adding a suffix, if the accent falls on the final syllable of the original word, has helped me to spell 'committed' accurately, but I also spell its sister word 'committment,' and I saw only this morning that a noted college professor of English does the same. Two words I admire and would use if I could spell them completely defeat me, and I have stopped using either 'exhortation' or 'exultation.' The same with 'forbear' and 'foretell,' not to mention 'forego' and 'foresee.'

I can differentiate between two words I favor, 'immanent' and 'imminent,' but whenever I use the former, some editor corrects it to the latter. I am invited to write forewords to many books; those doing the inviting spell it 'forward,' as does my secretary. She handed me a note the other day: 'Latest count, foreword 7, forward 13. The good guys are winning.'

Five words give me considerable trouble because they are so universally mispronounced I am almost tempted to believe they should be spelled 'nucular,' 'miniscule,' 'dimunition,' 'momenta' and 'infintesimal.' In fact, by this time next century those may have become the accepted pronunciations and spelling.

To pick my way through this jungle which no man ever masters completely, I keep at hand a valuable small book which gives merely the spelling of 25,000 basic words. Many such books are available, and a writer needs one. Mine is *Instant Spelling Dictionary* by Dougherty and Fitzgerald.

Having read so widely as a young man, what do I read now? Obviously, an enormous amount of research material, which is work, and not too many novels for pleasure. But I do listen to my peers as they discuss current writing and take note of what I should be reading whenever I face a long plane trip. Some time ago I read six novels by our best women writers, recommended by various friends: Sylvia Plath, Anne Rice, Joyce Carol Oates, Joan Didion, Toni Morrison and Judith Rossner. I have rarely been more rewarded, and wished that I myself might have written that delightful Gothic frolic, *Interview with the Vampire*, a clever updating of the Dracula myth. For my next spree: Thomas Berger, Mario Vargas

Llosa, Donald Barthelme, John Irving and Robert Coover.

In the unbroken chain of which I am a part, reading breeds writing, which breeds more reading. I have grave suspicions about young writers I meet who aspire to a life in the verbal arts without having done their homework in Balzac and Camus, Tolstoy and Pasternak, Dickens and Hardy, Melville and Cheever. How can they possibly evolve the standards which will enable them to compete?

WHO IS VIRGIL T. FRY?

———— ◇ ————

Originally published in The Clearing House *in October 1941, with a new* The Beginning *by James A. Michener written in 1993.*

The Beginning

*T*his short, short story played a focal role in my life. Look at its publication date, October 1941. I was thirty-four that year and had written nothing except academic materials which were published primarily because I was editor of the learned journals to which I submitted them.

For some reason I cannot now recall I decided to draft a short character sketch which would cut right at the heart of our nation's educational problems. I could visualize the subject of my story, for I had taught with him and had not particularly liked him. I thought he was prone to showboat. But I was also intelligent enough to know that he had teaching *capacities far beyond the prosaic ones I had developed.*

I submitted my story to a magazine which I did not edit. Although this educational journal had never before published fiction, the editors accepted my tale immediately, published it in the next issue, and launched it on a career that would last more than half a century and garner thousands of readers who could identify with the various characters.

It was the first piece of fiction I had written, and its enthusiastic reception gave me the first quiet intimation that perhaps I could write. But I did not allow its wide success to nudge me away from my academic writing. It would be 1944, three years later, before I would again try my powers on fiction, Tales of the South Pacific, *and eight years, 1949, before I would risk quitting my job as editor and taking the hazardous gamble of trying to become a free-lance writer.*

Look at how short the story is, hardly a foretaste of the long novels I would write. Look at how the action and the progression of ideas come from dialogue, an approach I would not emphasize in my later books. Look also at the crisp movement, the inviting nar-

rative style and the extreme simplicity of both words and sentences. They would reappear later as marks of my writing.

The significance of this first story, however, goes much deeper than style. I had spent much thought in constructing the name of my hero, Virgil T. Fry, and he acquired such vital life that he became a part of me. When marooned on a South Pacific island which war had passed by, I sought a naval officer around whom I could build the stories that I was hearing as I traveled from island to island. And mysteriously, like the rising of the sun after a long, dark night, the name Virgil T. Fry emerged, and I built my novel around him.

But, important though he was, curious misadventures befell him both in the novel and in the musical play that resulted from it. In the former I was writing about lusty, island-marooned sailors, and the name Virgil sounded completely inappropriate for those rugged characters. Every time I typed it I felt a twinge of impropriety. Eventually I abandoned it, adopting the strategy that his middle name was Tony, and then he sounded just right. There were Tonys in the Sea-Bees, and my man found a comfortable home there, becoming a principal character.

However, when Rodgers and Hammerstein fashioned the novel into a play, they dropped Tony Fry completely. Josh Logan, the famed director who co-authored the drama, told me why: 'Just before starting on your story I'd done Mister Roberts *by Tom Heggen, and your tale duplicated his, even though you wrote yours first. Roberts and Fry were both loners, they both won the love of their men, and they both died off-stage. Too damned much coincidence; he had to go.'*

So Virgil, my guiding star, was robbed of both his novel and his musical, but in my mind he lives on, for had I not created him so vividly in 1941 I might never have found a structure for my first professional writing in 1944. I salute him in both his manifestations.

Who Is Virgil T. Fry?

◇

I have never known a man more fascinating than Mr. Virgil T. Fry. His fascination grows daily because I have never met him.

Mr. Fry, you see, was my predecessor in a small Indiana high school. He was a teacher of the social studies, and he was fired for incompetency. I was brought in to take his place.

Dr. Kelwell, the superintendent of schools in Akara, first told me about Virgil T. Fry. "Fry," he said, "was a most impossible man to work with. I hope you will not be like him."

"What was his trouble?" I asked.

"Never anything in on time. Very hard

man to work with. Never took advice," was the reply. Dr. Kelwell paused and leaned back in his chair. He shook his head violently. "Very poor professional spirit." He nodded as if to agree with himself, then repeated, "I hope you won't be like him."

The principal, Mr. Hasbolt, was considerably more blunt.

"You have a great chance here," he said. "Mr. Fry, your predecessor, was a very poor teacher. He antagonized everyone. Constant source of friction. I don't recall when we ever had a teacher here who created more dissension among the faculty. Not only his own department, either. Everyone in this building hated that man, I really do believe. I certainly hope you won't make the same mistakes." He wrung my hand vigorously as if to welcome me as a real relief from a most pressing and unpleasant problem.

The head of the social-studies department in which I worked was more like Dr. Kelwell than like Mr. Hasbolt. He merely hinted at Mr. Fry's discrepancies. "Very inadequate scholar. Very unsound. Apt to go off half-cocked," he mused.

"In what way?" I asked.

"Oh—lots of ways. You know. Crack-pot ideas. Poor tact in expressing them. You have a real opportunity here to do a good job. I certainly hope you won't make Fry's mistakes."

But if the head of my department was in-direct, the head of the English department wasn't. "That man!" she sniffed. "He really was a terrible person. I'm not an old maid, and I'm not prudish, but Virgil T. Fry was a most intolerable person. He not only thought he could teach social studies and made a mess of it, but he also tried to tell me how to teach English. In fact, he tried to tell everyone how to do everything."

Miss Kennedy was neither an old maid nor prudish, and she was correct when she intimated that the rest of the staff felt as she did. Mr. Fry had insulted the music depart-ment, the science department, and above all the physical-education department.

Tiff Small was head of athletics. He was a fine man with whom I subsequently played a great deal of golf and some tennis. He wouldn't discuss Fry. "That pansy!" and he would sniff his big nose into a wrinkle. "Pretty poor stuff."

Mr. Virgil T. Fry's landlady ultimately became my landlady, too, and she bore out everything the faculty had said about her former boarder: "Never cleaned his room up. Smoked cigarettes and dropped the ashes. I hope you don't smoke. You don't? Well, I'm certainly glad. But this Mr. Fry, my he was a hard man to keep house for. I pity the poor girl that gets him."

Remembering Tiff Small's insinuation, I asked my landlady if Fry ever went with girls. "Him? He courted like it was his sole occupation. Finally married a girl from Akara. She was a typist downtown. Had been to the University of Chicago. Very stuck-up girl, but not any better than she had to be, if you want my opinion. Quite a girl, and quite good enough for Virgil T. Fry."

As the year went on I learned more about Fry. He must have been a most objectionable person, for opinion concerning him was unanimous. In a way I was glad, for I profited from his previous sins. Everyone was glad to welcome me into the school system and into the town, for, to put it baldly, I was a most happy relief from Virgil T. Fry.

WHO IS VIRGIL T. FRY?

Apart from his personality he was also a pretty poor teacher. I found one of his roll books once and just for fun distributed his grades along the normal curve. What a mess they were! He had 18% As where he should have had no more than 8%! His Bs were the same. And when I reached the Fs, he was following no system at all. One person with a total score of 183 was flunked. The next, with a total score of 179, had received a C! And in the back of his desk I found 247 term papers he had never even opened! I laughed and congratulated myself on being at least more honest than my predecessor, even if I excelled him in no other way.

I was in this frame of mind when Doris Kelley, the sixteen-year-old daughter of a local doctor, came into my room one evening after school. "May I ask you a question?" she said.

"Of course."

"Maybe you won't like it," she replied, hesitating a moment.

I laughed, "Certainly I will. What is it?"

"Why don't you teach the way Mr. Fry did?"

I was taken aback. "How did he teach?" I asked.

"Oh," was the answer, "he made everything so interesting!"

I swallowed and asked her to elaborate.

"Well, Mr. Fry always taught as if everything he talked about was of utmost importance. You got to love America when you got through a course with Mr. Fry. He always had a joke. He wasn't afraid to skip chapters now and then.

"He could certainly teach you how to write a sentence and a term paper. Much better than the English teachers, only they didn't like it very much. And did you *read books* when Mr. Fry taught you! Ten, maybe, a year, and all in the very kinds of things you liked best. Hitler, strikes, the Constitution, and all about crime. Just anything you wanted to read.

"And class was always so interesting. Not boring." She stopped and looked at me across the desk with a bit of Irish defiance in her eye.

She was a somewhat mature girl and I concluded that she had had a crush on this remarkable Mr. Virgil T. Fry. "Did all the pupils feel that way?" I asked her.

"I know what you're thinking," she said, smiling. "But you're wrong. Everyone liked him. Almost every one of them did. And the reason I came in to see you this evening is that none of us like the way you teach. It's all so very dull!"

I blushed. Everyone had been telling me what a fine job I was doing. I stammered a bit, "Well, Mr. Fry and I teach two different ways."

"Oh, no," she insisted, "it's not that. Mr. Fry really taught. He taught us something every day. I'll bet if you ask all the pupils they'll all say the same thing. He was about the only real teacher we had."

I became somewhat provoked and said a very stupid thing. "Then why was he fired?"

No answer.

"You did know he was fired, didn't you?"

Doris nodded.

"Why?" I repeated.

Doris laughed. "Don't you know? All the kids do." And she stood in the door, smiling. "Jealousy," she said.

I was alarmed. I wondered if the pupils really did dislike my teaching as much as Doris had implied. The next day in a class of which Doris was not a member I tried an experiment.

"Well," I said, "we've now reached the end of the first unit. I wonder if it wouldn't be a good idea to go back to a discussion of the big ideas of this unit?"

I paused.

Not much response, so I added: "The way Mr. Fry used to do?"

Immediately all the pupils sat up and started to pay attention. Most of them smiled. Two of the girls giggled and some of the boys squirmed. They obviously wanted to accept my suggestion. "Tom," I asked, "will you take over?" for I had no idea what Mr. Fry's method was.

Tom nodded vigorously and came to the front of the room.

"All right," he rasped, "who will dare?"

"I will," said a girl. "I believe that Columbus came to the New World more for religious reasons than for commercial reasons."

"Oh!" groaned a group of pupils, snapping their fingers for attention. Tom called on one.

"I think that's very stupid reasoning, Lucille. Spain was only using religion as a mask for imperialism."

Lucille turned in her seat and shot back, "You wouldn't think so if you knew anything about Philip the Second."

And the debate continued until Tom issued his next dare. A pupil accepted and defiantly announced: "I think all that section about Spain's being so poor at colonizing is malarkey. Everything south of Texas except Brazil is now Spanish. That looks pretty good to me."

I winced at the word "malarkey" and the pupils winced at the idea. The tigers of Anglo-Saxony rose to the defense of the text and the challenging pupil did his best to stand them off.

A few nights later I drove some other pupils to a basketball game in a nearby city. One of the boys observed, as we were coming home: "Class has been much better lately. I sort of like history now."

"How do you mean, better?" I asked.

"Oh, more the way Mr. Fry used to teach."

"Was Mr. Fry such a good teacher?" I asked.

"Oh, boy!" chortled the crowd, all at once. And one continued, "Was he? Boy, he could really teach you. I learned more from him than my big brother did at the university, in the same course. That's a fact! I had to read more, too, but I certainly liked it."

"I always thought he was rather—well, sissy?" I observed.

"Fry? Oh, no!" the boys replied. "It's true he didn't like the athletic department and used to make some pretty mean cracks about athletes, but we all liked it a lot. No, Mr. Fry was a very good tennis player and could swim like a fish."

The question of reading bothered me. I had always aspired to have my pupils read a great deal, and here they were all telling me that last year they had read and this year they hadn't. I went to see Miss Fisher, the librarian, about it.

"No," she said, "the books aren't going out the way they did last year."

"Could it be that maybe Mr. Fry knew how to use the library better?" I asked.

"Oh, no!" was the laughing reply. "You're twice the teacher Mr. Fry was. All the staff thinks so. He was a terrible person around a library!"

This depressed me, and I sought for an answer outside the school. I went around that night to visit Dr. Kelley, Doris' father.

"The fact is," he said, "you're in a tough spot. Virgil T. Fry was a truly great teacher. You're filling the shoes of a master. I hear the children talking at table and about the house. Fry seems to have been the only teacher who ever really got under their skins and taught them anything."

He paused, then added, "As a matter of fact, the pupils find your teaching rather empty, but I'm glad to say they think it's been picking up recently." He knocked out his pipe and smiled at me.

"Then why was Fry fired?" I asked.

"Difference of opinion, I guess," the doctor replied. "Fry thought education consisted of stirring up and creating. He made himself very unpopular. You see, education is really a complete social venture. I see that from being on the school board. Fry was excellent with pupils but he made a terrible mess of his adult relationships."

"You're also a father," I said. "Don't you

think your daughter deserves to have good teachers?"

He lit his pipe again. "Of course, if you want the truth, I'd rather have Doris study under Fry than under you. In the long run she'd learn more." He smiled wryly. "At the same time, what she learns from you may be better for her in the long run than what she would have learned from Fry."

"May I ask you one question, Doctor?" I inquired. He assented. "Did you concur in Fry's dismissal?"

Dr. Kelley looked at me a long time and drew on his pipe. Then he laughed quietly. "I cut board meeting that night. I knew the problem was coming up."

"How would you have voted?" I persisted.

"I think I would always cut board meeting," he answered. "Fry was a disruptive force. He was also a very great teacher. I think the two aspects balanced precisely. I would neither hire him nor fire him. I wouldn't fight to keep him in a school and I wouldn't raise a finger to get him out of one."

I frowned.

He continued: "The fine aspect of the

whole thing is that you, a beginning teacher, don't have to be all Fry or all yourself. You can be both a great teacher and a fine, social individual. It's possible."

Dr. Kelley laughed again as he showed me to the door. "Don't worry about it. And you may be interested to know that your superintendent, Dr. Kelwell, feels just as I do about the whole problem. He stood out till the last minute to keep Fry. Very reluctant to have him go."

I went home badly confused, and I have remained so ever since.

As I said before, I have never known a man so fascinating as Mr. Virgil T. Fry. Not a member of his faculty has a good word to say for him and not a pupil in any of his classes has an unkind word to say against him.

VERSES TO A WRITER
HEADING FOR NINETY

——— ◇ ———

Poem by James A. Michener
written in Austin, Texas
in July 1993.

photo by John Kings

Verses

To a Writer Heading for Ninety

We see him in the twilight and the setting
  of the sun,
Hiking by to greet us when our working
  day is done.
  Leaving his garden where squirrels
    come for food,
      He walks our tree-lined paths
      And climbs our little hills,
The dogs greet him with fond
  solicitude.

    Night after night in rain or sultry heat
    He makes his way along our quiet
      street
      And throws a cheery smile
      To those by chance he meets.

My little sister used to watch
Each night to see him pass
And wondered why he strode along our
    road:
    'Have you no bed to go to when
    'The stars tell us to sleep?'

He smiled at her and smoothed her
    hair:
    'I climb the hills to give my heart
    'A task to make it work
    'So that I sleep at night and rise
    'Again at dawn once more to strive
    'At deeds I dare not shirk.'

'Did you have fun today?' she asked
And he said: 'I enjoy each day
    'And what it cares
    'To bring my way.
    'The rain or the storm or starlit nights,
    'I love them all.'

I sought the secret of this wanderering
    man
And spied upon him as he passed our
    way,

But when I questioned him he had no
   plan,
And seemed content with any random
   day.
    'At night I see your light
    'When you get up to write
    'Why do you work so hard?'
And he replied: 'I have a double goal.
  'I work so hard to exercise my heart,
  'I write so much to activate my soul.'

    He huffed and he hobbled
    On paths that were cobbled
Till I was afraid he might fall.
    But he was defended
    By those he'd befriended
And he wasn't worried at all.

Three runners stopped beside him
   Before they passed him by:
'Why do you come to test this track
'Old man? You'll wrench your back!'
   He smiled: 'If you keep running
   'As you do these tranquil nights,
'Perhaps you'll have the strength as I
'To thus your ninety years defy.'

Each time he passed she met him with a
smile,
A crippled woman with a damaged brain:
'I'm glad to see you hike your steady
mile.
'It's good to hear that you're at work
again.'
She vaguely understood he published
books
And badgered him for one to show the
town.
He'd see her in the mall in quiet nooks,
His book in hand, but reading upside
down.
He thought, 'I deem we're judged by how
we use
'Whatever gifts we are vouchsafed by
God.
'Allowed my brain, she might have
reached the stars.
'Entrapped by hers, I'd leave my paths
untrod.'
For her he merely marks the end of day.
For him she flames a beacon for his
way.

Young people came to talk with him
    From India and Spain,
And when they left they lugged their
    bags
    Of books with lighter air.

It seemed these youths his steps would
    vitalize.
'When you are old like me you spend your
    nights
'In wondering from where new talents
    will arise
'To dream new dreams and serve as
    acolytes.
    'To take your place
    'When you have left.
'Much work remains for dedicated
    hands
    'And searching minds.
'The world cries out for leadership
    'Who will it find?'

'Is that the reason you are out at night,
'Searching the streets to find a lad of
    worth
'To take your place?' And he said: 'No.

157

'I come to watch the fading light
'Of day that warmed the earth
'To hear the singing of the twilight birds
'To see gold shadows on the moon's pale
face.
'For if the world stays right
'Young men and women blessed with
thoughts like mine
'Will rise to sing the songs and write the
books
'And feed the squirrels too when I am
gone.'

And then he sang this song:
'O Earth, how fortunate I am
'To have plumbed your secrets in fullest
measure
'And known so well your glorious
treasure
'Your burning sands
'Your coraled strands
'Your turbulent seas
'Your verdant leas
'Volcanos with their molten fire
'Fulfillment of the heart's desire.
'An open road with light in distant dark,

'And strength to travel it when young
'And memories when youth is sprung.

'That's why I walk these cobbled paths so
  patiently each night.
'A man who searches steadfastly will
  sometimes find the light.'

OPINIONS
ON OTHER
WRITERS

◇

ERNEST HEMINGWAY

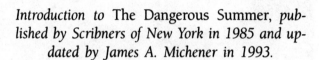

Introduction to The Dangerous Summer, *published by Scribners of New York in 1985 and updated by James A. Michener in 1993.*

Ernest Hemingway

*T*he *Dangerous Summer* is a book about death written by a lusty sixty-year-old man who had reason to fear that his own death was imminent. It is also a loving account of his return to those heroic days when he was young and learning about life in the bull rings of Spain.

In the summer of 1952 *Life* magazine headquarters in Tokyo had dispatched a courier to find me with the troops along the front lines in Korea with an intoxicating message. After prowling the mountainous terrain along which desultory action was taking place, he located me at a forward post with a small detachment of Marines.

"*Life* is engaged in a tremendous venture," he told me in conspiratorial whispers. "We're going to devote an entire issue to one manuscript. And what makes the attempt so daring, it's fiction."

"By who?"

"Ernest Hemingway."

The name exploded in the cavelike foxhole with such force, such imagery, that I was instantly hooked. I had always admired Hemingway, considered him our best and certainly the man who had set free the English sentence and the crisp vocabulary. As I wandered about the world I constantly met foreign writers who went out of their way to assure me that whereas they considered themselves as good as Hemingway, they did not want to mimic him. They had their own style and were satisfied with it. And I began to wonder why they never said: "I don't want to write like Faulkner . . ."—or Fitzgerald, or Wolfe, or Sartre, or Camus. It was always Hemingway they didn't want to copy, which made me suspect that that's precisely what the lot of them were doing.

If you had asked me the day before that meeting with the *Life* man I'd have said: "I admire Hemingway immensely. He gave us all a new challenge. But of course I don't want to write like him."

The emissary continued: "With so much riding on this experiment *Life* can't afford to take chances."

"On Hemingway? How could you lose?"

"Apparently you haven't been following the scoreboard. The critics murdered his last offering."

"*Across the River and Into the Trees?* It wasn't too hot. But you don't condemn an artist for one . . ."

"That's not the point. They not only blasted the novel, which was pathetic, but they called into question his legitimacy, his right to publish any further."

"I can't believe that."

"Didn't you read that savage burlesque of him and his novel? That hurt."

"I missed it, being over here. But you can't burlesque a man unless he's very good to begin with . . . unless readers are so familiar with his work that they catch the jokes. You don't waste your time teasing a nothing."

"This wasn't teasing. This was a thrust at the jugular."

"Hemingway probably told them to go to hell."

"Maybe, but he was deeply hurt. And *Life* is painfully aware that the attacks cast a shadow over whatever he publishes next." The man paused to study the battlefield in front of our dugout, then came to the point: "We have one hell of a bundle—money, prestige—riding on this one-shot issue."

"Why come to see me?"

"We want to present the story in the best possible light."

"What can I do? I don't know Hemingway."

"Do you respect him?"

"He's one of my idols."

"That's what the editors hoped." He looked me in the eye, then said: "They want you to read the galleys . . . make up your own mind . . . no pressure from us. And if you like what you see, give us a statement we can use in nationwide publicity."

"To what purpose?"

◇

"To kill any lingering reminders of those savage reviews. Knock in the head suspicions that the old man might be through."

"Tell me the truth. Have you asked other writers better known than me? Have they refused?"

"I really don't know. But I do know the editors think that your approach to war and the role of men makes you eligible. Also, they think readers will listen."

"Is Hemingway in on this?"

"He would be mortified if he knew we thought we needed help. He'll know about it when he sees the copy."

The decision was easy and automatic. I assured the emissary that I would read the manuscript, praying that it would be good, and if it was I would not hesitate to say so boldly. Because a writer just getting into his career as I then was rarely has an opportunity to pay tribute to one of the masters.

"Guard this with your life," the emissary said. "This is the only copy outside New York. And if you decide to make a statement, get it to us in a hurry." Placing the rather frail parcel in my hands, he nodded, warned me not to leave it where others might spy, and left to catch the Tokyo plane.

The next hours were magic. In a poorly lighted corner of a Marine hut in a remote corner of the South Korea mountains I tore open the package and began reading that inspired account of an old fisherman battling with his great fish and striving to fight off the sharks which were determined to steal it from him. From Hemingway's opening words through the quiet climaxes to the organlike coda I was enthralled, but I was so bedazzled by the pyrotechnics that I did not trust myself to write my report immediately after finishing.

I knew that Hemingway was a necromancer who adopted every superior Balzacian trick in the book, each technical device that Flaubert and Tolstoy and Dickens had found useful, so that quite often his work seemed better than it really was. I loved his writing, but he had proved in *Across the River and Into the Trees* that he could be banal, and I did not want to go out on a limb if he had done so again.

But as I sat alone in that corner, the galleys pushed far from me as if I wished to be shed of their sorcery, it became overwhelmingly clear that I had been in the presence of a masterpiece. No other word would do. *The Old Man and the Sea* was one of those incandescent miracles that gifted writers can sometimes produce. (I would learn that Hemingway had dashed it off in complete form in eight weeks without any rewriting.) And as I reflected on its perfection of form and style I found myself comparing it with those other gemlike novellas that had meant so much to me: Edith Wharton's *Ethan Frome*, Joseph Conrad's *Youth*, Henry James' *The Aspern Papers*, and Faulkner's *The Bear*.

When I had properly positioned Hemingway's tale among its peers I hid the galleys beneath my bedroll and walked out into the Korean night, agitated by this close contact with great writing, and as I picked my way across the difficult terrain I made up my mind that regardless of what critics sager than I had said about Hemingway's previous fumbles, I would have to flaunt my opinion that *The Old Man* was a masterpiece, and to hell with caution.

I am embarrassed to state that I have no record of what I actually reported. My judgment appeared in full-page ads across the country, and I think I said something about how happy writers like me were that the champ had regained the title. No one reading my words could doubt that here was a book worth immediate reading.

At any rate, *Life* used my statement enthusiastically and paid me, but what I didn't know was that while their Tokyo agent was handing me my top-secret copy of the galleys—"the only set outside New York"— *Life* was distributing another six hundred sets to opinion-makers across the United States and Europe, each one top secret and unique. When the issue containing Hemingway's novella appeared during the first week of September 1952 it was already an international sensation. One of the cleverest promotions ever orchestrated had resulted in immediate sales of 5,318,650 copies of the magazine, the swift rise of the book version to head the best-seller list, and a Nobel Prize.

Hemingway had won back the championship with a stupendous ninth-round knockout.

* * *

The success of this daring publishing venture had a surprising aftermath. *Life* was so pleased with its coup that the editors decided to try their luck a second time, and when they cast about for some writer who might do another compact one-shot, they remembered the man who had stuck his neck out when they needed a launching statement for their Hemingway.

Another emissary, this time from New York with lots of corporate braid, came to see me, in Tokyo I believe, with a dazzling proposal: "We had such an unprecedented success with *The Old Man* that we'd like to go back to the well again. And we think you're the man to do it."

"There aren't many Hemingways around."

"On your own level you might do it. You understand men in action. You have any stories in the back of your mind?"

I have always tried to answer such questions forthrightly. I love writing. I love the swirl and swing of words as they tangle with human emotions. Of course I had a dozen ideas, most of them worthless when inspected closely, but a couple of them seemed to have real staying power.

"I've been doing some combat flying over Korea."

"At your age?"

"And a lot of patrol work on the ground. I see certain big outlines."

"Like what?"

"Like it's perilous for a democracy to engage in war without declaring war. Like it's morally wrong to send young men into action while old men stay home and earn a bundle without any war taxes or deprivations. And it is especially wrong to call a few men arbitrarily into action while allowing others just as eligible to stay home free."

"Would your story be beating those drums?"

"I don't beat drums."

"Write it. I think we might have something."

Driven by a fire I had rarely known, and excited by the prospect of following in the shoes of Ernest Hemingway, I put aside all other work. On 6 July 1953 *Life* offered its second complete-in-one-issue novella, *The Bridges at Toko-ri*. This was less than a year after the great success of *The Old Man* and, as before, the editors protected themselves

by asking another writer to authenticate the
legitimacy of their offering. This time they
chose Herman Wouk to say good things, and
although I cannot remember what I said
about Hemingway, I recall quite clearly
what Wouk said about me: "His eyes have
seen the glory." That became the sales pitch
this time, but a friend of mine writing a review for the *New York Herald Tribune*
phrased it more cautiously:

> This is, says an advance publicity
> release, "the first major work of fiction
> to be written expressly for *Life*." We are
> not sure whether they mean they
> *ordered* a major work of fiction from
> Mr. Michener, who duly complied, or
> that the novel happily turned out to be
> a major work of fiction after it was
> completed. We are not even sure, for
> that matter, whether it *is* a major work
> of fiction.

Although the sales of my effort did not come
close to matching those of Hemingway's, the
second try was sufficiently rewarding to
start the editors looking for a third and a

fourth successor, thinking that this could become a yearly ritual. I believe they planned to keep the daisy chain going: me to applaud Hemingway's effort, and then write my own; Wouk to applaud mine and then to write his, and whoever cheered Wouk to write the fourth. Alas, Wouk had nothing in the works that he wished to throw into the race, so *Life* hit upon a British writer with a reputation almost equal to Hemingway's, but his novella fell on its face disastrously, and Number Four was abandoned. *Life's* one-shot innovation worked sensationally with a vintage Hemingway. It was moderately acceptable with someone like me, and a flop if the writing was not both inspired and compact. The experiment died.

I met Hemingway only once. Late one wintry afternoon in New York my longtime friend Leonard Lyons, columnist for the *New York Post* and a sometime confidant and traveling companion of Hemingway's, called me: "Papa's up from Cuba. We're here with Toots. Come on over."

When I reached the famous bistro I found Shor in his favorite corner dispensing insults: "Imagine a man of my substance wastin' a whole day with this bunch of writin' creeps." Hemingway, Lyons, and two gofers whose names I did not catch were trading war stories, and although Leonard had assured me that Papa wanted to see the man who had stuck his neck out in defense of *The Old Man*, Hemingway made no mention of that fact; indeed, he was so self-conscious and rude that he even refused to acknowledge that I had joined the party.

Two exchanges softened him. At one point he said, referring to my hometown: "I never wanted to be known as 'that gifted Philadelphia writer.' I wanted to go up against the champions, Flaubert, Pío Baroja." He was astonished when I said that I had once paid my respects to Baroja, a down-to-earth novelist whom I held in great regard. Shortly before Baroja's death, Hemingway had told the salty old man: "You deserved the Nobel Prize, not me." And we spoke affectionately of this hardgrained Spaniard.

More surprising to Hemingway was the fact that I had once traveled with a cuadrilla of Mexican bullfighters, and he was delighted to learn that I had known the

Mexican greats: Juan Silveti with his cigar, fearless Luis Freg, drowned in a boat accident in Mérida, Carnicerito de Méjico, killed in the bull ring, the superb Armillita with no chin and never a major goring, the gaudy Lorenzo Garza, the engaging Silverio Pérez.

We spent some time with these matadors, Hemingway condemning most of the Mexicans to second category, but then I happened to mention the Spaniard Cagancho, the flamboyant gypsy whom Hemingway had respected for the man's unashamed cowardice. This led to a discussion of the corridas I had seen in Spain as a university student on vacation, and when he learned that at my first fight in Valencia—Domingo Ortega, Marcial Lalanda, El Estudiante—I had fallen under the spell of Ortega, a dour, hard fighting man, he told Toots: "Any man who chooses Domingo as his hero knows something," and I told him: "When I was last in Madrid for San Ysidro, Ortega was advisor to the presidente and remembering me from when I trailed along behind him he invited me to join him in the palco."

Hemingway nodded approvingly, but he could not bring himself to thank me for what I had said about *The Old Man*, nor did I wish to bring up the subject. Not long after, in July 1961, I heard that he was dead at the age of sixty-one.

The last extended work of any importance that Hemingway wrote was another assignment for *Life*, and one can visualize the clever editors of that magazine at some strategy session in 1959 proposing: "Wouldn't it be great if we could get Hemingway to bring his bullfighting book up to date?" All present, remembering the great success *Life* had had with *The Old Man*, must have jumped at this suggestion, and when it was presented to Hemingway he must have liked it, too.

In 1930 he had published in *Fortune* a longish, knowing article on bullfighting as a sport and an industry and this led, two years later, to the remarkable illustrated essay *Death in the Afternoon*. A disaster with the critics, who could not understand why a writer of his talent should waste himself on such arcane material, it quickly became a cult book.

Those of us who liked bullfighting recognized this as a loving, faithful, opinionated account of an art form which few non-Spanish speakers understood. We applauded his daring in bringing it to an indifferent public, and we knew it was destined for a long subterranean life. It was one hell of a book.

Succeeding decades had seen it climb to respectability, with Scribners selling hundreds of thousands of copies and reprinting it dozens of times. As bullfighting became popular, with several motion pictures of merit gaining it new adherents, *Death in the Afternoon* became a kind of Bible, with library aficionados who had never seen a fight ardently debating the relative accomplishments of Belmonte, Joselito and Niño de la Palma. I had kept the book with me in Mexico when I traveled with bullfighters.

In 1959 Hemingway went back to Spain and during that long, lovely summer when he was already beginning to suffer the ravages which would in the end destroy him—monomania about being spied upon, suspicion of his most trusted friends, doubt about his capacity to survive—this powerful man, so much a legend of his own creation, returned to the vibrant scenes of his young manhood. With great good luck he arrived in Spain just as two wonderfully handsome and charismatic young matadors, brothers-in-law, were about to engage in a protracted mano a mano, hand-to-hand duel, which would carry them and their partisans to most of the famous bull rings in Spain.

The matadors were Luis Miguel Dominguín, thirty-three years old and usually the more artistic, and Antonio Ordóñez, twenty-seven, the brilliant son of Cayetano Ordóñez (who fought under the name Niño de la Palma), whom Hemingway had praised in *Death in the Afternoon*. Fairly matched in skill and bravery, they were sure to put on a stupendous show. It proved to be a glorious summer, a most dangerous one, and Hemingway adopted that concept for the title of his three-part series, *The Dangerous Summer*.

Certain facts about the manuscript he produced are significant. *Life* had commissioned him to write a crisp, 10,000-word article about what it was like to go back, but he became so obsessed by the drama of the summer—much of which he superimposed upon a solid base—that he was powerless to halt the flood of words. The first draft ran to 120,000 words. The polished manuscript, from which the *Life* excerpts and the present book were edited, ran to about 70,000. The present version, which contains about 45,000 words, endeavors to give the reader an honest rendering of what was best in this massive affair.

I cannot be critical of the vast amount of overwriting Hemingway did—120,000 words when 10,000 were all that was needed—because I often work that way myself. I have consistently turned in to magazines and newspapers three to four times the number of words requested, prefaced by the note that will accompany these pages when I submit them to Scribners:

> You are invited to edit this overlong manuscript to fit the space available. You are well-regarded editors and cutting is your job.

Even in the writing of a novel I persistently write more than is required, then cut back toward the bone. When a recent publication asked me for six sharp pages on a pressing topic, I warned them: "In six pages I can't even say hello. But I'll invite you to cut."

I wish I could have heard what went on in *Life's* editorial offices when they saw what their request for 10,000 words had produced. A friend once sent me a photostat of a marginal note which had appeared on one of my submissions to a different magazine: "Somebody ought to tell this son-of-a-bitch that he's writing for a magazine, not an encyclopedia."

What *Life* did was to employ Hemingway's good friend and traveling companion A.E. Hotchner to edit the manuscript, cutting it ferociously. Intended originally as a one-shot nostalgic essay, it would appear as a three-part extended account of the peripatetic duel between the two matadors. I have been permitted to see Hemingway's original version of Part II of the *Life* series and can say with certainty that no magazine could have published the entire version. No book publisher would have wanted to do so either, because it was redundant, wandering in parts, and burdened with bullfight minutiae. I doubt if there will ever be a reason to publish the whole, and I am sure that even a reader who idolizes the author loses little in the present version of the book. Specifically, I think Hotchner and the editors of *Life* did a good job in compressing Hemingway's outpouring into manageable form, and I believe that the editors of Scribners have done an even better job in presenting the essence in this book.

I was in Spain following the bulls shortly after the *Life* series appeared under the agreed-upon title *The Dangerous Summer*, so I was in a position to evaluate its acceptance by the international bullfighting public, a suspicious, envious lot. Men and women alike took strong stands, and the consensus seemed to be: *It was great that Don Ernesto came back. He reported the temporada enthusiastically. He was too partial to his favorite boy. And he should be stood against the wall and fusilladed for the things he said about Manolete.*

It is generally agreed among bullfight fans that the two greatest matadors of recent history have been Juan Belmonte, the twisted little gnome of the 1920s, and Manolete, the tall, tragic scarecrow of the 1940s. Some add the Mexican Carlos Arruza, dead before his time, and bobbysoxers and tourists from France deem the recent phenomenon El Cordobés worthy of inclusion, although purists dismiss him with contempt because of his excessive posturing.

For an American outsider like Hemingway, no matter his long service to the art, to barge into Spain and denigrate Manolete was like a Spaniard sticking his nose into Augusta and claiming that Bobby Jones did not know how to play golf. I heard some extremely harsh indictments, including threats in the tapa bars to beat up on Hemingway if he dared to show his face, but as time passed the castigation became less severe until even Manolete's partisans acknowledged that to have had a Nobel premiado like Hemingway treat their obsession seriously, and in a magazine of *Life*'s circulation, was a desirable thing. Don Ernesto was re-enshrined as the patron saint of the art.

More serious, I think, was the charge that in reporting upon the mano a mano between the brothers-in-law Hemingway had abused the position of the writer by siding so outrageously with one of them, Ordóñez, whom he knew best and obviously idolized. Again and again he betrayed his partisanship—which was justified by the awesome performances of his man—in sentences that an impartial reporter should not have used: "I do not know what Luis Miguel (Dominguín) did nor how he slept the night before the first decisive fight at Valencia. People told me he had stayed up very late but they always say things after something has happened. One thing I knew; that he was worrying about the fight and *we* were not."(My italics.)

Long after publication of the articles, Hemingway confessed that he had not treated Dominguín fairly and half-apologized, but the damage had been done. This book stands as an unwarranted attack on Dominguín, who was not as outclassed in that long duel as Hemingway claims.

The articles had not been in circulation long when rumors began to reach us that *Life* considered their publication a disaster. Readers were impatient with the long digressions that not even Hotchner's careful editing could eliminate. The newness that had greeted *Death in the Afternoon* was replaced by a jadedness which caused readers to mutter: "We've read all this before." We were assured, erroneously it turned out, that *Life* had actually halted the series in midflight because the reception had been so negative, and we heard other reports, accurate we found later, that Hemingway himself was disgusted with the whole affair, for he realized belatedly that he had made a mistake in doubling back in the first place and in writing so copiously in the second. Representatives from *Life* admitted that they were not entirely happy with the way it had turned out. The text did not appear in book form, and Hemingway was understood to be happy when the matter died an unlamented death. An aficionado from Bar Choko said: "This time it was death in September."

My own judgment, then and now, was that Hemingway was unwise to have attempted this return to his youth; that he tried to hang far too much on the slender, esoteric thread of one series of bullfights; but that he produced a manuscript that revealed a great deal about a major figure of American literature. It is a record worth having.

To the lover of taurine literature, Hemingway's description of the historic Málaga corrida of 14 August 1959 in Chapter 11 is one of the most evocative and exact summaries of a corrida ever penned. It is a masterpiece. That afternoon the brothers-in-law fought an exceptional set of Demecq bulls, and the fame of the corrida still reverberates, because the two men cut ten ears, four tails and two hooves. There had never before been such a performance in an arena of category.

Hemingway could have ended his manuscript on that high note, but because he was an artist who loved both the drama and the twists and turns of the arena, he ended his series with a corrida of much different quality, and on its tragic heroic note he ended what he had to say about the two men whose footsteps he had dogged like a starstruck little boy.

To those, and they are legion and of good sense, who will protest that Hemingway should have wasted so much attention on a brutal affair like bullfighting, or that a major publisher should resuscitate his essay, or that I am defending the work, I can only say that many Americans, Englishmen and Europeans generally have found in the bullfight something worthy of attention. That one of our premier artists chose to elucidate it both in his youth and in his older age is worthy of note, and I have never been ashamed to follow in his steps.

Bullfighting is far less barbarous than American boxing, and the death of men comes far less often, in recent years something like sixty deaths in the boxing ring to one in the bull ring. And few Americans are aware that our football, high school and college, kills a shockingly higher number of young men than bullfighting and makes paraplegics of scores of others.

Of course, bullfighting has elements of brutality, but so does surgery, hunting and the income tax. *The Dangerous Summer* is an account of the brutal, wonderful challenging things that happened during one temporada in Spain. Since *The Dangerous Summer* focuses on bullfighting and its participants, both in the ring and in the stands, it is essential that the reader understand and perhaps even try to appreciate the marvelous rituals governing this art form, this elaborately choreographed dance of death.

Publisher's Note: At this point Mr. Michener provided sixty-two compact paragraphs of erudite description of the bullfight, composing what amounted to twenty-two pages of technical terms. He and Scribner's had decided this glossary was needed to make Hemingway's descriptions meaningful to the reader. The present publishers, producing this book for a different group of readers, felt this long discourse was not needed and sought Mr. Michener's permission to cut. He demurred: 'Bullfighting has been of major importance to me. I've written about it in Iberia *(1968) and used it as a major theme in* Mexico *(1992). It dominates my short book* My Lost Mexico *(1992) and is the sole material of my illustrated novella* Miracle in Seville *(to be published in 1994). These pages are vital to me, so let's keep them.' Further discussion, over several months, convinced him that cutting was advisable.*

Hemingway's essay in its present book form will be treasured by two special groups of people. Devotees of American literature who revere Hemingway, of whom I am one, will find a confused farewell from a great and legendary figure. We witness his curious behavior toward his wife when he adopts various attractive young women during the feria at Pamplona. We see the longing with which he returns to those singing woods near Roncesvalles. We come suddenly upon his own assessment of *The Sun Also Rises*: "I've written Pamplona once and for keeps."

Certain passages reverberate with the authentic Hemingway touch: "[We] ... stopped at the next town where two storks were nesting on the roof of a house where the road made a dropping bend. The nest was half built, the female had not laid her eggs yet and they were courting. The male would strike her neck with his bill and she would look up at him with storklike devotion and then look away and he would stroke her again. We stopped and Mary took some photographs but the light was not too good."

We get many insights into Hemingway's character, his bravado, his preoccupation with death, his intolerance toward inferiors, his wonderful generosity when he identified with someone he deemed worthy of respect. In these years he met two young American friends of mine, John Fulton, a Philadelphia boy who aspired to be a bullfighter, and Robert Vavra, a California lad who wanted to be an animal photographer. Listening to their stories, he impulsively drew from his wallet a check which he signed for one hundred dollars. When they tried to thank him, all he could say was: "Buena suerte."

But he could also be miserably aggressive. When he met another friend of mine, Matt Carney, who knew more about bulls than Hemingway, he goaded the young man into agreeing to a fist fight and then withdrew before any blows were exchanged.

The Dangerous Summer is instructive regarding a minor brouhaha that involved his friend A. E. Hotchner. Some critics, resenting the way in which Hotchner appeared to have appropriated Hemingway, accused him of being a fancifier. One extremely harsh article that appeared in *Atlantic* magazine after the publication of Hotchner's book *Papa Hemingway* even made me begin to wonder whether Hotchner had ever known the master. This manuscript, and the photographs which appeared with the *Life* articles, prove not only that Hotchner knew Hemingway intimately but also that Hemingway trusted and relied upon him. I was glad to have this clarification.

I cherish the throwaway paragraphs in which Hemingway reminds us of the sparse way he worked and of his refusal to use commas: ". . . I went into the cage of a wolf which had been recently trapped on the place and played with him which pleased Antonio. The wolf looked healthy and the odds were all against him having hydrophobia so I figured all he can do is bite you, so why not go in and see if you can work with him. The wolf was very nice and recognized someone who liked wolves."

Most such treasurable bits have been retained, and they provide affectionate glimpses of the man and the writer. On the other hand, the purely bullfight passages have been sharply cut, so that the devout aficionado will miss details which he would have savored. Both the *Life* editors and those responsible for the present volume decided—properly so, I judge—to eliminate from most of the corridas the names and work of the matadors other than Dominguín and Ordóñez. But someone like me, knowing the matadors thus eliminated and their histories, regrets the loss of revealing paragraphs like the following:

There were two other matadors on the bill that afternoon. "Miguelín" a short bushy-headed local boy and fearless clown and Juan Garcia "Mondeño" a tall, spare, grave, boy with a serenity, calmness and controlled purity of style who fought his bulls as though he were serving Mass in a dream. He was the best new bullfighter I saw last year.

Miguelín was the same comic figure, but a little more unpleasant. He treated the bulls with an insolence and contempt they had no way of returning and he knew enough and had good enough reflexes to spread his bad taste and his clowning contempt for everything that made bullfighting worth watching like some nasty syrup over the ring. He did everything but chew bubble gum when he passed a bull. He was a home town boy and his neighbours loved it.

Pepé Luis's second bull was difficult and also weak in the legs. He made excellent isolated passes with cape and muleta and tried to get something out of the bull then quit and gave up.

The local boy Francisco Anton "Pacorro" was justifiably cautious with his first bull which was very dangerous and hooked on both sides. His feet jittered away on purpose, at the start. Then he could not control them and it looked for a while as though the bull would go out alive. His townspeople were merciless with him especially all those in the sun who, if they could have controlled their own feet, would have been bullfighters. . . .

On the last bull, which was good, he did everything on his knees to control the nerves that made his feet jump away. Once he had them under control he stood up and worked the bull beautifully with the old and classic passes. He went in beautifully to kill but hit bone hard. This upset him and he went back onto both knees to pass the bull again. The bull caught him on the ground, tossed him high in the air and he came down sprawled like a rag doll and obviously wounded.

He shook off the people who tried to hold him, squared the bull with the muleta and went in to kill in a rush. The bull came out dead from the encounter and swayed over. They carried Pacorro into the callejón and out under the stands to the infirmary. The ears and tail followed him into the operating room while we were making our way out through the crowded callejón, past where the bulls were being butchered to the cobbled patio of the picador's horses where the cars were parked.

I could read reminiscences like that for hours, but I do confess that whereas aficionados like me have lost something through the cutting, the typical reader has not. Indeed, a plethora of such material—and there are long pages of it left on the cutting floor—would so alienate the general public that the manuscript would probably never be finished by most readers if it were published intact.

The taurine reader will want to know what happened to the conqueror Ordóñez after his incandescent triumphs during that dangerous summer of 1959. In subsequent years I saw him fight perhaps two dozen times and invariably he was disgraceful. Although others saw him fight well after 1959, the times I saw him he was pudgy and evasive, apparently terrified of any real bull he faced. He took refuge in every ugly trick that Hemingway despised, accomplishing nothing with cape or muleta and killing with a shameful running swipe from the side.

And yet we crowded the arenas to see him, hoping in vain for one final afternoon of honest triumph. It never came. Instead we saw debacles, heard boos and whistles, ducked as cushions came showering down upon him, and watched as the police prepared to rescue him if outraged fans tried to invade the arena. Hemingway was spared these indignities. He had traveled with Ordóñez when the matador was incomparable, and it was of this greatness that he wrote.

MARGARET MITCHELL

———— ◇ ————

Introduction to the Anniversary edition of Gone With the Wind, *published by Macmillan in 1975, the 75th anniversary of Margaret Mitchell's birth.*

Margaret Mitchell

Within the space of eighty-nine years, four novelists from four widely divergent national literatures published books focused on a new type of heroine: free spirited, attractive, immoral and totally ingratiating.

In 1847 in England, William Makepeace Thackeray offered the first of these unforgettable portraits, Miss Becky Sharp of *Vanity Fair*.

In 1857 in France, Gustave Flaubert related the banal yet tragic events engulfing *Madame Bovary*.

In 1875 in Russia, Leo Tolstoy unfolded a long and majestic portrait of Anna Karenina and her associates.

And in 1936 in the United States, Margaret Mitchell published a novel which was to have a shattering impact, *Gone With the Wind*, centering upon the fortunes of Scarlett O'Hara. A few comparisons will help the reader already familiar with these books to appreciate their relationships.

The three male authors were proved, professional literary talents when they published their books. Margaret Mitchell was an untested housewife living in what each of the European authors would have described as "a provincial city."

It is notable that Thackeray, Flaubert and Mitchell published their books when they were thirty-six years old. Tolstoy, having published *War and Peace* at that watershed age, did not publish *Anna Karenina* till eleven years later, when he was forty-seven.

The four books are alike in that they deal with liberated women, but Emma Bovary and Anna Karenina, faced by the consequences of their radical deportment, commit suicide. The novels named after them are classic tragedies. Becky Sharp and Scarlett O'Hara survive and, indeed, prosper. Their books, not named after them, are certainly not tragedies and might best be considered comedies of manners.

Vanity Fair, Anna Karenina and *Gone With the Wind* deal essentially with the upper classes of their societies, often with compassionate side glances at the state of the peasantry. Because of this, they sometimes seem outmoded today, focusing as they do upon the gentry. *Madame Bovary*, on the other hand, makes a specific virtue of dealing with an average French village and its population.

Anna Karenina and *Gone With the Wind* have the virtue of dealing with a great nation in time of crisis and gain added strength and interest because of their wide historical scope and relevance. The other two works lack this breadth.

Artistically each of the books has its unique virtues, which account for the high regard in which it is held. For pure literary control few novels in any genre have ever equaled *Madame Bovary*; its crystalline purity remains a standard and an enchantment. For comic invention few novels excel *Vanity Fair*; its style of expression may have fallen from fashion, but its sardonic insights never will. *Anna Karenina* has a magisterial quality, its many characters offering variation and challenge. And *Gone With the Wind* displays high skill in its interweaving of narrative passages describing historical events and dramatic scenes in which characters confront one another. To achieve a satisfactory balance between narrative and scene is a major obligation of the novelist.

Psychologically each writer displays a clear vision of his or her central character. Flaubert has been excessively praised for his analysis of Emma Bovary, but she is observed within a limited range of situations and emotions. Tolstoy did a splendid job on each of his four major characters, but Thackeray tended to gloss over his. Margaret Mitchell had great success with Scarlett O'Hara, less with Rhett Butler; but of the four major women in this assembly of novels, it is Scarlett who lives most vividly and with greatest contemporary application.

Frank, in common with all men he knew, felt that a wife should be guided by her husband's superior knowledge, should accept his opinions in full and have none of her own. He would have given most women their own way. Women were such funny little creatures and it never hurt to humor their small whims. Mild and gentle by nature, it was not in him to deny a wife much. He would have enjoyed gratifying the foolish notions of some soft little person and scolding her lovingly for her stupidity and extravagance. But the things Scarlett set her mind on were unthinkable. That sawmill, for example. It was a shock of his life when she told him with a sweet smile, in answer to his questions, that she intended to run it herself.

Structurally the novels of Thackeray and Tolstoy fall apart in their final pages, the former disastrously so, as if Thackeray had no clear understanding of what he was about, the latter because Tolstoy was trying to force his story of Anna into a larger mold to which it was not suited. (In the final nineteen chapters Anna cannot appear, for she has already committed suicide; indeed, she is scarcely spoken of by the characters who survive). *Madame Bovary* holds together beautifully, like a Greek tragedy, but this is because Flaubert is working on a very restricted canvas not likely to provide any tempting diversion. Miss Mitchell's very long novel, however, offers many temptations for the author to go astray, but she keeps it vital, relevant and interesting right up to the last page. In her ability to devise and control an intricate dramatic structure, she excels the other three by far.

In critical acceptance, judging these novels alone, Flaubert stands supreme with Tolstoy not far behind. This is partly because these two presented their portraits as tragedies, which the public has been trained to accept as a higher level of art. Thackeray has been much diminished in recent years because of his flippancy, his outmoded style and his lack of high intention, but I would expect his fortunes to revive. Margaret Mitchell was excessively praised at publication, numerous critics comparing her novel favorably with *War and Peace*, and was excessively deflated in the 1950s and 1960s because of her parochial viewpoint and the lack of development in her characters. I am certain that her reputation will grow in the future, because critics will have to grapple with the problem of why her novel has remained so readable and so important to so many people.

Popular acceptance was accorded each of the first three novels. Thackeray became the sensation of London; Tolstoy was already the glory of Russia. However, it was *Gone With the Wind* which the entire world would embrace.

It is difficult even now to comprehend what a staggering event *Gone With the Wind* was in that post-depression year of 1936. Today a good novel that sells 40,000 copies can lead the best-seller lists, and a sale of 200,000 copies is a veritable sensation. So great was the word of mouth publicity on *Gone With the Wind* that within twenty days of publication 176,000 copies had been sold. Over the summer months, when bookstores customarily fell into doldrums, sales rose to 700,000 copies, one New York store ordering 50,000 on one day. Within a year of publication, 1,383,000 copies had been sold. Today, sales stand at about 21,000,000.

The impact on American society was

memorable. Appearing at the end of a Depression during which many families had faced great loss, this story of a saucy French-Irish girl of sixteen facing up to the Civil War and holding her family together through the post-war reconstruction became more than a mere novel. It became a symbol. Editorials were written, pointing out the relevancy. Sermons were preached in churches across the nation directing parishioners to lessons learned. Politicians used the novel as an allegory pointing the way to national survival. And individual readers wrote thousands of letters to Miss Mitchell, assuring her that in this novel they read the story of their own lives.

The Macmillan Company, which had the good fortune to publish the book, saw to it that a constant stream of interesting stories circulated. One woman, leaving New York on a boat trip to Europe, found that she had received nine copies as bon-voyage presents. A maiden lady in Boston who had never been south of the Hudson River started reading the novel one morning and kept at it through the night. When her Boston *Transcript* landed on her porch next afternoon, she staggered to the door, looked out with bloodshot eyes and cried, "Get out of here, you damned Yankees!"

For two years Miss Mitchell lived at the center of a publicity spotlight more fierce than that known by any writer since the day on which Lord Byron could say, after publication of *Childe Harold*, "I awoke one morning and found myself famous." Newspaper publishers and magazine editors besieged her, praying for any scrap of writing. She was offered fantastic sums if she would write even a portion of a page, on any subject that came to mind. Wherever she went she was encircled by people begging autographs. Every worthy cause in the South implored her to make a statement or an appearance in its behalf. Uncounted invitations to speak piled in. The pressures became almost intolerable.

Then, in 1938, the pace accelerated. Hollywood had purchased her novel, at the ridiculously low figure of $50,000 for all movie rights, and a great publicity brouhaha was generated over which actors and actresses were best qualified to play the leading roles. The heady nonsense that ensued might have derailed a weaker person, but with unwavering determination Miss Mitchell kept herself clear of it. She would participate in no sensationalism. If she had been a practiced author, with a score of earlier books to her credit, her sagacious behavior under such pressure would have been remarkable. For an untested young woman to receive such adulation on her first book, and to accept it with such stately restraint, was a miracle.

I met Miss Mitchell twice in those hectic years. I was a minor editor at Macmillan and my cubbyhole stood next to the second-floor office of Mr. Brett, head of our company. I remember the awe with which word flashed through our rooms that "Margaret Mitchell is coming in for lunch today!" We waited with more than ordinary respect, because we were aware that the generous Christmas bonuses we had been receiving were due solely to the profits she had made possible. I remember an official of Macmillan's telling me, "It was Mr. Brett who made one of the significant decisions in American publishing. At our final meeting on price we showed how this very long book could just possibly be published at the traditional price of two dollars and fifty cents . . . if it turned out to be a big success. It would be safer, however, to publish at the radical price of two seventy-five. Mr. Brett leaned back in his chair and asked, 'Can this book be as good as everyone says?' We told him yes and he said, 'If it's that good, people will want it. The price is three dollars.' "

My secretary called excitedly, "Here she comes!" And I went to my door to watch as the solemn procession, much like the marching priests in *Aida*, moved past. There was Mr. Brett the young and impulsive head of our company, and Harold Latham the stout and gracious head editor, and Alec Blanton the charismatic businessman, and Jim Putnam the Oxford-type gentleman editor, all surrounding a very tiny woman, not five feet tall and weighing much less than a hundred pounds. The four men looked fiercely protective, aware of the gravity of this day, but Margaret Mitchell looked from side to side, nodding to the secretaries and the junior editors. I thought then, and I would like to think now, that when she

The Great Novel of the South!

GONE
WITH
THE
WIND

by

MARGARET MITCHELL

A superb story of love and heroism, laid in one of the most glamorous periods of the nation's history, filled with living, breathing people, packed with tense action and exciting adventure.

"The book is absorbing. It is a fearless portrayal, romantic yet not sentimental, of a lost tradition and a way of life."—ELLEN GLASGOW

"This book has been waiting to be written for many years."
—HENRY SEIDEL CANBY *{Book-of-Month News}*

"The most satisfactory, most convincing, most powerful presentation of the period that has ever been put into fiction."

—PAUL JORDAN-SMITH

The Book-of-the-Month
for July

1037 pages $3.00

Advertisement for *Gone With the Wind*

reached my cubbyhole she smiled with special graciousness.

Later that day, and on her second visit, I was allowed to shake hands with her and I could not get over how small she was. One of the Macmillan men whispered to me, "When she attends a formal dinner she takes along a copy of *Bartlett's Quotations*. Puts it on the floor so her feet can touch."

I have often thought, in recent years, of those queenly visits and what happened to the participants. Marvelous Alec Blanton, the certain hope of the publishing industry, dead in an unfathomable suicide. Gentlemanly Jim Putnam, moved on to a good job in another company. George Brett, gone from the historic company, which he sold. And Margaret Mitchell, killed in one of the most senseless tragedies in American literature. Gone with the wind, all of these.

Certain myths associated with the novel ought to be dispelled, and the seventy-fifth birthday of the author is an appropriate time to do so.

That Margaret Mitchell was a simpleminded Atlanta housewife who fumbled her way into the writing of a famous novel. False.

She came from a distinguished Atlanta family, all of whose members read widely. At ten she was writing novelettes and plays which astounded her contemporaries. She inclined toward vigorous dramatization and conscripted a repertoire company of neighborhood children who acted out her writing. In her *Phil Kelly, Detective*, she played the role of "Zara, a female crook and one of the gang." She attended Smith College in Massachusetts, then landed a job on the *Atlanta Journal*, where she followed in the footsteps of Laurence Stallings, Grantland Rice and Roark Bradford. She was an alert, street-smart, irreverent, popular little reporter who married a typical southern sharpie, then had the good sense to divorce him almost immediately.

That she was a naive woman who was hoodwinked by smart New York publishers. False. Her father and brother were smart lawyers and legal scholars who checked every clause in her contract. Her second husband was a knowledgeable businessman who gave her excellent advice.

That scores of publishing houses read and rejected her novel before Macmillan grudg-

ingly accepted it. False. It took Margaret Mitchell ten years to write her novel, and during most of that time she had as her close personal friend Lois Cole, Macmillan's representative in Atlanta. Miss Cole sent repeated brief notices that a very clever young woman in her territory was in the process of writing a novel which might be good. Harold Latham, Macmillan's senior editor, looked Miss Mitchell up during a scouting trip to Atlanta, and was the first professional publisher to see the material. The manuscript was in dreadful physical condition and was almost the size of its author. Latham crammed it into a large suitcase he purchased for that purpose and carried it off with him, but Miss Mitchell, having fears that he might think it unsuitable, telegraphed him: SEND THE MANUSCRIPT BACK. I'VE CHANGED MY MIND. Prudently, he refused. Instead, he sent her word that Macmillan wanted to publish it. At that time the novel was called *Tomorrow Is Another Day,* and it was not until just prior to casting the manuscript into type that its heroine's name was changed from Pansy O'Hara to Scarlett.

That Miss Mitchell, being a woman and Southern to boot, could not possibly have written such a novel; it was done by some male friend. False. It is true that prior to her death she directed that her manuscript and all papers related to it be burned, and this was done; but a few sample pages, research notes and other documents were put aside to prove, should the need ever arise, that she alone had written the novel. On this point the testimony of brother, husband, editor and proofreader is overwhelming.

That the book is merely another Civil War novel. False. The book contains 947 pages and 63 chapters. The Civil War ends on page 444, in the first sentence of Chapter 29. The remaining pages and chapters deal with post-war events, and these are often the most interesting and provocative. Thus 54% of the pages and 56% of the chapters are not, strictly speaking, Civil War. In time span the same is true. The first 28 chapters deal with events occurring between the dates of April 1861 and April 1865. The last 35 chapters deal with the years 1865–1873. Scarlett is sixteen when the book opens, twenty-eight when it closes.

That the book was copied from Vanity Fair. I think that anyone informed in world literature would have to notice the parallelism between Scarlett O'Hara-Melanie Hamilton and Becky Sharp-Amelia Sedley, and in the first major review of the book, by J. Donald Adams in the *Sunday New York Times Book Review,* this similarity was pointed out, as it should have been. But Miss Mitchell was firm in rejecting the imputation:

> I see that Scarlett, the central character, is coming in for comparison with Becky Sharp. Nothing could be more flattering but the fact remains that I never read *Vanity Fair* till about a year and a half ago, after my auto accident. When I read *Vanity Fair* at last, I was charmed beyond words and howled with delight; but it never occurred to me that there'd be a comparison between Becky and Scarlett.

Actually, the analogy with *Vanity Fair* is not the most apt, for Thackeray's two women do not have associated with them men as inter-

217

esting or as important as those in *Gone With the Wind*. A much more appropriate comparison is with Anna Karenina, for here the analogous structure is almost identical. Anna and Vronsky are extremely similar to Scarlett and Rhett, while the lovely Princess Kitty Scherbatskaya and her rural husband Konstantin Levin are dead ringers for Melanie Hamilton and Ashley Wilkes. Miss Mitchell never commented on this parallelism, for it seems unlikely that she had read Tolstoy's masterpiece. However, almost any novelist depicting a woman like Scarlett would want to counterpoise against her a woman like Amelia or Kitty or Melanie. Honoré de Balzac had done just this in 1841 when he wrote what may have been the progenitor of all these novels, his delightful *Memoirs of Two Young Married Women,* in which an impetuous Louise follows a stormy path strewn with handsome men while the more sober Renée finds matronly happiness with her more stodgy lover, who winds up a count. But I doubt that sources for *Gone With the Wind* need be sought elsewhere than in the mind of an impressionable child listening to family recollections of the Civil War and its aftermath.

The essential fact about this novel, however, is its extraordinary readability. May Lamberton Becker, a major critic when the book was published, delivered the permanent verdict: "It is the shortest long novel I have read in a long time." It is filled with stunning scenes: Mammy lacing Scarlett into her corset; the wounded at the railway station; Scarlett shooting the Union straggler; the girls making Scarlett a dress from the moss-green velvet draperies; Rhett carrying his wife upstairs to the long-unused bedroom.

But the novel does not depend merely upon superdramatic confrontations. Contrary to what some critics have argued, the two major characters do grow—Melanie and Ashley do not—and I have always felt that the central paragraph comes toward the middle of the book, in Chapter 29:

Somewhere, on the long road that wound through those four years, the girl with her sachet and dancing slippers had slipped away and there was left a woman with sharp green eyes, who counted pennies and turned her hands to many menial tasks, a woman to whom nothing was left from the wreckage except the indestructible red earth on which she stood.

In the final pages there is a similar portrait of Rhett at forty-five:

He was sunken in his chair, his suit wrinkling untidily against his thickening waist, every line of him proclaiming the ruin of a fine body and the coarsening of a strong face. Drink and dissipation had done their work on the coin-clean profile and now it was no longer the head of a young pagan prince on new minted gold but a decadent, tired Caesar on copper debased by long usage.

Primarily, however, it is the South that changes, altered by war and defeat and social upheaval and stark determination to reestablish itself. The abiding merit of this novel is not that it has given us the portrait of a headstrong young woman, but that it has depicted with remarkable felicity the spiritual history of a region.

The book's weakness is that it focuses so uncompromisingly on Atlanta, ignoring the rest of the South, the nation and the world. One is struck, when reading Miss Mitchell's private letters, by her obsession that the better class of people in Atlanta should like her book. This led her to a highly restricted view of Negro liberation and permitted her to offer a paragraph like this; she is speaking, not a character:

The former slaves were now the lords of creation and, with the aid of the Yankees, the lowest and most ignorant ones were on top. The better class of them, scorning freedom, were suffering as severely as their white masters. Thousands of house servants, the highest caste in the slave population, remained with their white folks, doing manual labor which had been beneath them in the old days. Many loyal field hands also refused to avail themselves of the new freedom, but the hordes of "trashy free issue niggers," who were causing most of the trouble, were drawn largely from the field-hand class.

A more comprehensive and compassionate view of freedom was possible, but she ignored it.

Finally, the book contains many single sentences and paragraphs which positively sing. Some are extravagant; some are nineteenth century in style; but all add to the essentially romantic quality of this much-loved novel:

She thought wildly: Let the whole Confederacy crumble in the dust. Let the world end, but you must not die! I couldn't live if you were dead!

Hunger gnawed at her empty stomach again, and she said aloud: "As God is my witness, as God is my witness, the Yankees aren't going to lick me. I'm going to live through this, and when it's over, I'm never going to be hungry again. No, nor any of my folks. If I have to steal or kill—as God is my witness, I'm never going to be hungry again."

He swung her off her feet into his arms and started up the stairs. Her head was crushed against his chest and she heard the hard hammering of his heart beneath her ears. He hurt her and she cried out, muffled, frightened. Up the stairs, he went in the utter darkness, up, up, and she was wild with fear.

It is with a sense of deep personal loss that I write this paragraph. On August 11, 1949, Miss Mitchell, who had been born in the opening year of this century, was walking across Peachtree Street to attend a movie, *A Canterbury Tale*, when a taxicab, running wild, struck her brutally, knocking her into the gutter. Five days later, without regaining consciousness, she died. The driver was found to have a record of twenty-four arrests for speeding, recklessness, disorderly conduct and other violations. On the day after his trial he was involved in yet another crash.

It seems highly doubtful that Margaret Mitchell, had she lived, would have written other books. An editor at Macmillan who knew her well told me prior to her death that she had indicated to him that she would not, and we have various letters in which she stated positively that she would write no more: "As you can gather from my novel, I'm a verbose creature, but I feel that nothing short of insanity will ever make me write another line." She is best considered, I think, a unique young woman who before the age of ten loved to tell stories and who at twenty-six began a long and powerful recollection of her home town. That it was destined to become a titanic tale of human passions, loved around the world, was a mysterious marvel then and remains one now.

MARCUS GOODRICH

———— ◇ ————

Afterword to a reprint of Delilah *by Southern Illinois University Press in 1977 and updated by James A. Michener in 1993. Delilah was originally published by Farrar & Rinehart in 1941.*

photo courtesy of Helene Goodrich Horner

Marcus Goodrich

In the bleak days of World War II when the American fleet lay hiding or at the bottom of Pearl Harbor, the United States government issued a frantic call for men to staff the new navy that must come into being if the nation were to survive. I was among the inept civilians who responded—ribbon clerks, school teachers, bulldozer operators—and like the others I knew practically nothing about the Navy, but a judicious Annapolis man gave me the needed advice: "If you want to understand what it's all about, read the novel that came out last year. It's called *Delilah*, and when you finish, you'll know what a ship is."

From reading reviews during the first weeks of 1941 I had become aware that such a book had been published and was being acclaimed, but I could not have anticipated that it was to play a crucial role in my life. Like hundreds of other new-fledged Navy men, I now read it with growing astonishment; it was so powerful, so uncompromising in its depiction of what happens in a fighting ship that I was stunned by its brilliance.

I shall never forget the awe with which I read that focal passage beginning, "There is a notable [tower] on a flat plain between Marseilles and the Spanish Border. . . ." With the aid of this tower, the author spelled out his theory of civilization: that society erects towers along its frontiers—floating towers called ships, if the sea is involved—and mans them with the toughest, most resolute defenders it can find. The exits are then barred, and the men are required to protect their tower, inch by inch, retreating if necessary from one prepared position to another, until at last they fall with the final parapet "if they had been what the tower intended." In glowing sentences that reverberated like the echoes of a battleship's guns, the author then told of the tower at Aigues Mortes which had been defended by such men, and of the Alamo, of which he says, "Thermopylae had its messenger of defeat. The Alamo had none."

Upon this solid base the author constructed a yarn of life aboard a rackety overage destroyer, and when he finished we beginners comprehended what kind of enterprise we had joined. Few novels ever appeared at a moment when they were so needed; *Delilah* became a tower of defense in those perilous opening days of our Pacific War. It carried a sense of destiny, as if the author had anticipated, a generation earlier, that what he was bursting to say was needed. I doubt that I have ever read another novel which so precisely fulfilled my requirements at a given moment, and scores of other Navy men felt the same, for from it we learned the traditions of our fleet:

No crew has ever gotten as far as a mutiny in the American Navy. Once, eighteen years before the War Between the States, a forgotten Midshipman and two Seamen attempted to incite one aboard the *Somers*. The Captain and the rest of the crew promptly hanged them at the yard-arm, despite the fact that the Midshipman was a son of the Secretary of War.

But what we learned most was that when we entered the Navy, and especially one of its ships, we surrendered ourselves into an archaic world governed by rules that would normally have been incomprehensible. In Goodrich's splendid phrase, we were now part of "an intact anachronism."

(2)

Because many would-be readers of this powerful novel, which I obviously like for its realistic depiction of life at sea, tell me that it is almost impossible to find a copy for sale, I think it best to provide a brief glimpse of how radically it is structured.

It's a long book, 496 pages in a period when 275 was about the average for a first novel, focusing on the doings aboard a rusty, over-age American destroyer commissioned

in 1900 and now, in 1916, preparing for re-
tirement. Its regular beat is the Sulu Sea,
that remote and dramatic arm of the western Pacific, bounded on the north and east
by the Philippine Islands, on the south by
rugged Borneo and on the west by elongated
Palawan, again a part of the Philippines.
The Sulu, one of the world's romantic bod-
ies of water, has always been frequented by
pirates from mainland China to the west,
and its shores have been the scene of almost
unceasing religio-military warfare. Its north-
ern shores are populated by Christian Tagalogs, its southern by Muslim Moros. The
Sulu was a sea ordained for beat-up rust
buckets like *Delilah* and her catch-as-catch-
can crew.

The novel is composed of three related but
not interwoven segments, each of which
could have been published separately as self-
standing novellas, one brief, one average, and
the last very long. It has no central plot, no
conspicuous development of character, and it
builds to no sensational denouement. It is a
collection of adult observations about men at
sea and it ends, like many voyages, just about
where it began. But its narration is so rich,

its concepts so varied, and its language so beautiful that it provides a rare reading experience regardless of its subject matter or tenuous plot.

The first episode, requiring only thirty-five pages, reports on how *Delilah* conducts herself while on a mercy mission in 1915 or 16 to that perpetual trouble spot, Zamboanga, at the southern end of the Sulu Sea. Two enlisted men who will appear frequently throughout the book, Water-tender O'Connel, the massive heavyweight champion of the squadron, thirty-four years old, and Signalman Warrington, a reticent bookworm out of Texas, seventeen years old, help fire the rusting boilers. And when the forced run is completed, an Irish monk who has spent thirty-five years in the islands, climbs nonchalantly ashore to decelerate a Muslim uprising.

The second episode requires 151 pages and relates the bizarre events surrounding a wild-goose chase up the uncharted western shore of Palawan Island in search of a reported underground river being used by Japanese military adventurers. This is a beautiful, haunting segment in which nothing much happens except the establishment of a mood and the presentation of additional crewmen.

The third episode covers 303 pages and could have been offered as a novel complete in itself, for it is more varied in detail than what has gone before. During a wild shore leave at Cavite, *Delilah's* men take on the whole fleet. Sharks invade a dry dock with disastrous results. Two long flashbacks deal with missionary problems, one in China, one in the Philippines. A submarine blows up. And O'Connel goes on one of the best-described rampages in literature; he carries a silver plate in his head following heroic events for which he won the Congressional Medal of Honor, and what happens to him in his shore-and-sea explosion is both real and moving.

The novel ends with exactly the right touch: a dispatch from Washington informs the *Delilah* that the United States is now at war with Germany—this is April 6, 1917—so that the harsh, unruly, confused and willing men who have been whipping themselves and their over-age destroyer into condition can see that they are needed. But there are no heroics. Chief Boatswain's Mate Crutch knows what steps will now have to be taken and in what order: "All right, you guys, get them boats up." The book ends. The war lies ahead.

I have always been partial to the episodic novel, because it seems to me that life and business and education and war proceed by episodes; and I have been suspicious of those other novels which wrap everything up in final packages. I was therefore disposed to like *Delilah*, and I remember the feeling of satisfaction that came with the closing pages, for I suspected that the way in which I was about to participate, and the ships in which I would serve, would involve unfulfilled episodes much like those reported in this novel, and I was impatient when some of my companions felt cheated by the drab ending of the book. But these disagreements did not tarnish our high regard for the novel; we recommended it to our friends and shared with them our reactions. And all of us became inquisitive about the author.

MARCUS GOODRICH

(3)

MARCUS AURELIUS GOODRICH was born in 1897, descendant of a family distinguished in Texas history. His father and mother were full cousins and sent their son to the public schools of San Antonio. From childhood he was familiar with legends of the Alamo, in whose defense one of his ancestors had died. After high school he joined the Navy in time to see, from his post on the Asiatic Station, the start of United States participation in World War I, a war throughout which he served mostly in the Mediterranean and the Atlantic. At war's end he attended Columbia University, moonlighting first as a big-city reporter, and then as stage manager for various Broadway productions. Later he landed full-time employment with a series of the finest newspapers of that time, and progressed to Paris as a correspondent for New York's *Theater Magazine* and the *New York Times Sunday Edition*, which enabled him to knock about the saloons of Europe with the Ernest Hemingway gang. Back in New York, he came to know many of America's leading literary figures, among whom he developed a reputation as a bon vivant, a compelling raconteur, and a young man destined for some notable achievement . . . if he ever got down to work. Clifton Fadiman wrote of him:

> The greatest taleteller I ever listened to is a man I used to know some ten years or twelve years ago, when the world was young. His tales were always of violent action overlaid by a passionate emotion. He held his audience mesmerized not only by the tensity of his fantastic narratives but by an extra infusion of feeling with which he charged that suspense. Above all things he wanted to be a writer, but none of us was convinced he ever would be. He was, we thought, too good a talker. He saved nothing for the writing desk. I knew vaguely that he was at work on a long novel. As the years passed, publication was postponed again and again, and my conviction was, with regret, reinforced—the conviction that Marcus Goodrich would never finish that book.

When the book appeared, it created a sensation. Front-page reviews were ecstatic. Word-of-mouth, as I can attest, was both vigorous and enthusiastic, and Goodrich became an overnight celebrity. What was equally encouraging, average readers gave the book high marks and began to speak of Goodrich as if he were a proud new voice in American letters. Few writers start their careers so auspiciously.

In the lead review in the *New Yorker* Fadiman said generously of his former drinking companion: "I don't know whether the book is worth the decade its composition has required—that's entirely the author's affair—but I am certain it is a remarkable work of art. . . . If 1941 gives us a better first novel by an American, it will be a year of miracles. . . . It cannot fail to make its author's reputation." (Goodrich would later explain that he spent not one decade writing *Delilah* but two.)

Lincoln Colcord, in a front-page review, said: "This is to hail a rather unusual phenomenon—a serious, full-length novel of the sea by a new author, and a novel that easily passes muster as a work of litera-

"Make way for Marcus Goodrich"
—FADIMAN, New Yorker

Page 1
N.Y. Times
Book Review
Feb. 2nd

Page 1
N.Y. Herald
Tribune Books
Feb. 2nd

The news IS

DELILAH

BY *Marcus Goodrich*

"I expect this is the novel of the year." —FRED T. MARSH, *N. Y. Times Book Review*

"A work of literature... a born story teller at the helm." —LINCOLN COLCORD, *Herald Tribune Books*

"If 1941 gives us a better first novel by an American, it will be a year of wonders." —CLIFTON FADIMAN, *The New Yorker*

Third printing

496 PAGES · $2.75

FARRAR & RINEHART · 232 MADISON AVE., N.Y.

ture. . . . In the course of its rambling narrative it furnishes a succession of incidental stories of the raw and tragic side of life that are told with vivid imagination and extraordinary power."

Fred T. Marsh, in a long and beautifully composed review for the *New York Times*, compared *Delilah* with *Moby Dick*, and concluded: "I expect this is the novel of the year. More important, I think, is the fact that here is something really good, something fresh even though traditional, something ancient though as timely as tomorrow's convoy."

William McFee, himself a masterful writer on the sea, to whom I shall return shortly, said: "The writing is magnificent. . . . It is the first time, so far as I know, where the personnel of a fighting ship of the United States has been treated with something of the fastidious fussiness that Proust used in his interminable novel." Other reviewers suggested comparisons with Joseph Conrad.

There were, of course, minority reports. Harry Sylvester pointed out that the callow, simplistic reactions of the sailors reminded him of the Rover Boys. Otis Ferguson in the *New Republic* said: "I hardly think it will go down as sea literature." E.B. Schriftgiesser said in the *Boston Transcript* that he for one would not await the second volume with enthusiasm; Robert Littell said in the *Yale Review* that reading it made him long for the blue editorial pencil; and even Fadiman confessed: "It is overwritten in spots and charged at times with a theatricalism that misses its mark."

But the consensus was that in Marcus Goodrich, America had found a major figure. I certainly thought so and remember how delighted we Navy men were when Goodrich became a national figure, capping it by marrying one of the most beautiful women in the world, the young actress Olivia de Havilland, fresh from her triumph in *Gone With the Wind.*

Photographs from that period show him as a slim, thoughtful man with receding light brown hair and an author's pipe jutting from the right corner of his no-nonsense mouth. He was, I thought, exactly what a successful writer ought to be. And then, mysteriously, he vanished.

In 1941 I had found *Delilah* to be a splendid novel. Thirty-seven years later the editor of this series has invited me to study it anew, a most gratifying experience, for I find that in the main my original assessment was accurate. It remains a remarkable work, harsh, uncompromising, intellectually severe, and most handsomely written. However, since its appearance three major wars have intervened—World War II, Korea, Viet Nam—and our national attitudes toward men and ships have altered drastically. And since I am no longer a beginning Navy man hungry for details about my new job, my reactions to *Delilah* have matured. It is a privilege to state them, for I owe this book a substantial debt.

I am impressed by the high sincerity with which Goodrich tackled his job back in 1920 when he first thought of writing about men at sea. It is quite apparent that he intended composing a great novel and that he was not going to be sidetracked by diversionary incidents or colorful characters, no matter how inviting. Did he succeed? Because of a peculiar contretemps which I shall discuss later, he never brought his master work to completion, so we can judge it only as a truncated effort. There it stands, incomplete, not wholly satisfactory, but a massive effort meriting our applause because of the obvious quality of its aspiration and the excellence of the half that has been completed.

This excellence is achieved by the use of various easily identified literary devices: rich allusion, adroit use of simile and metaphor, sustained passages of impassioned composition, arbitrary use of arcane words rarely found in normal discourse, protracted psychological analysis of motive and action, flashbacks which reveal character, and a liberal use of symbolism.

I was struck by Goodrich's wide-ranging allusions. Within the first few pages he reminds us that a place like the Wardroom of the *Delilah* had been sacred on ancient ships, a repository of gods. Sailors on patrol reincarnate "those raging Gothic squads, depicted in old woodcuts, about to roar through the shattered gate of a city." Men singing evoke the memory of a Mexican crowd. A sailor's wet hair hangs down evenly, like that of a Japanese. The watches the men stand are the same used on Agamemnon's hollow ships. Because fighting men manned their towers well, Aristotle was free to found science, Giotto to paint and Dante to write his poetry.

I try to avoid simile myself, and also metaphor, primarily because I am no good at them, but I can be envious of the skilled manner in which Goodrich uses both. The tranquility of the Sulu Sea has a malignancy "like that which pervades a brilliant stalk of bananas in which lurks an aroused tarantula." A Malay baby lying on his father's brown chest is "like a chocolate blossom." And the very effective comparison of the crew's bringing their ship into Cavite when no one on shore gave a damn: "They were like a college football player who, falling into the idea that he was in a vital game, had run seventy miraculous yards with a broken rib, only to find, when he staggered up to be helped heroically off the field, that the stands contained not a single person."

Goodrich's habit of introducing erudite words is almost always effective, so much so that I was not aware that this was his stylistic habit until I had nearly finished the book. Then, in a cursory review, I found such words as *rubefacient, impendence, obliviously, effluence, motile*; but I failed to locate half a dozen others whose meaning not even scholars could decipher. In no instance did I find Goodrich's partiality for the unexpected word irritating or in any way impeding my reading; in this respect he is much like John Updike or James Gould Cozzens, two writers whose love for words embellishes their stories with a richness that others of us fail to attain.

Of Goodrich's narrative devices, the only one that seemed outmoded by the novels that have intervened was his use of psychological analysis. From things he said after the book was printed he clearly fancied his long analyses of the amorphous relationship between Executive Office Fitzpatrick and signalman Warrington. When compared to similar work being done now, Goodrich's labored passages seem almost tedious; the best of our young contemporaries would dispose of this matter in a few powerful, revealing pages. Yet even in my disappointment I had to remember the stir made back in 1941 by these radically new passages: "a style which is a sort of Melville-out-of-Hemingway creation with a dash of Proust."

The flashbacks—perhaps we should call the first an arbitrary diversion—interested me enormously. In the first, Goodrich informs us as to how Ensign Woodbridge ran into trouble with missionaries when detached from the *Delilah* and placed in temporary charge of a gunboat up one of China's rivers. This is splendid story-telling, effective, evocative, delightful to the reader and a welcomed excursion away from the drab routine of the destroyer. And it is handled with just the right parsimony of word and incident. I commend this excellent passage to would-be novelists.

I was less enthusiastic about the long flashback—thirty-eight pages—dealing with the uncomprehending monster Parker; this seemed to suffer from all the extravagances which endanger this device: wordiness, contrived situations, unclear purpose and a perilous loss of forward motion in the narrative. Indeed, it seemed like a set piece, and for me it didn't work. And yet I saw the structural necessity for it: the monk had been used effectively in the first episode and for architectural reasons he must be brought back in the closing scenes. (I must be fair; Fadiman said of this same passage: "There is one set piece—the story of the monk and fiendish Mr. Parker, whom nothing but music could subdue—which has, I fear, nothing at all to do with the novel but which Conrad or Maugham would have given a finger or so to have written.")

Goodrich's use of symbolism, however, is skillful and not belabored. The blistering engine room into which Warrington must go is the fiery hell that boys traverse before they become men. The lost river is the Holy Grail that voyagers seek in vain. The sharks that invade the floating dock are the negatives that lie in wait beyond the rule of reason. And the laconic declaration of war reveals the hidden goal toward which men and ships move unknowingly. Because these concepts work, they give the novel its sense of destiny.

In the technical construction of this novel Goodrich was both clever and artistic. The relative weight of the three segments was exactly right. (I deem the opening episode one of the finest pieces of writing about the sea ever published; it compares with Joseph Conrad's *Youth* or the best of Herman Melville. The subtle juxtaposition of the brute O'Connel and the frail old monk is brilliant, as is the contrast between the creaking, boiler-bursting destroyer and the soft calm of the Sulu Sea.)

I have great respect for the long flashback, for it comes close to disaster, yet is saved by the sheer brilliance of the author's use of language. I like writers who risk long episodes like this, for when the passage succeeds, it reminds me of the difference between a writer and one who is not. A writer is a woman or man so possessed by an urge to communicate that he or she is willing to risk losing the reader altogether in order to lay forth an experience which the writer knows is viable, whether he can express it in congenial terms or not. On this reading I had admiration, and some envy, for the great first episode, for it succeeds completely; but I had respect for the second, because it is very daring storytelling which, though steering close to disaster, escapes it.

Artistically, this is an impressive book. It

should be compared, I think, with James Gould Cozzens' magisterial comedy, *Guard of Honor*, which deals with men at war with a similar honest detachment and analysis. In 1949 Cozzens won the Pulitzer Prize for this novel; in 1941, the year *Delilah* appeared, the judges made no award and how they missed this strong, prophetic book has remained a mystery.

I compare it also to that fine maritime novel, William McFee's *Casuals of the Sea*, which offers a powerful portrait of the merchant navy in much the same vein as *Delilah*. If a young person was eager to apprehend America's abiding relationship to the sea, and the background for adventures in the sky, he or she ought to read *Moby Dick*, *Casuals of the Sea* and *Delilah*, and the mystery would be laid open, for these are novels of which any sea-faring country could be proud.

Delilah may be more dated than the other two. A Navy man reading it today is astonished at how far away in time 1916 was! The crew of this destroyer seem like men from another century; their sentimental attachment to their ship rings strange on the ears of one educated in Viet Nam. When Ensign Snell was knocked flat during the coaling of the destroyer, Bos'n Cruck leaped to his assistance and raised him to his feet "in the impulsive response to the unproclaimed but almost religious tradition that an officer, like a flag, must never remain fallen." In Viet Nam a major problem for many officers was that in the confusion of battle disgruntled enlisted men were prone to toss live fragmentation grenades at the backs of their officers, if the latter got too far out in front. "Fragging the bastards," it was called.

The brutality practiced aboard the *Delilah*, and the manner in which the officers encouraged it in order to test their men, seem almost prehistoric. The young Jew Mendel had to be careful where he walked, because O'Connel liked to slug him in the belly just for the hell of it, and Mendel had no recourse. Time and again in reading of the 1916 Navy I found myself thinking: No wonder enlisted men at the conclusion of World War II insisted that the code for military conduct must be revised. The *Delilah*'s officers, line and petty, would rather sink their ship than adhere to the new code.

The contemporary reader will also find the blatant racism somewhat difficult to take. The men of the *Delilah* despise Jews— "A Jew had no business being a naval officer ... their guts were sour ... no iron in them"—consider the Japanese a "tricky, semi-savage people," and hold the Tagalog inhabitants of the Philippines beneath contempt.

The anti-Semitic passages gave me real trouble, and I went back again and again to try to unravel their significance. I have learned to my sorrow that readers tend to attribute to the writer of a book every expression of opinion it contains, even those voiced by characters obviously intended to be unsavory; this is one of the burdens of writing. So I was prepared to excuse Goodrich as being the mere author of those passages, and not their philosophical sponsor, especially since he later describes the deaths of his two Jews, Mendel and Schiff, as acts of great heroism.

But even when I granted this concession, the totality didn't seem right, and I reflected that Goodrich was in the Navy during those years when it was fearfully anti-Semitic; one

Annapolis yearbook printed the graduating photograph and record of its lone Jewish midshipman on a separate page with no printing on the back and perforated so that it could be torn out. In this way the young officers could own classbooks undefiled by Jewish taint. I did not know what to think.

Goodrich apparently experienced the same confusion, for many years later he wrote in a letter to a friend:

But the original version of the explosion aboard the submarine was another matter. There was something wrong about it, and it took me years to understand what it was. That episode was written in the nineteen twenties. Anti-Semitism was strong in the Navy then, and I was a product of my time. The story of that heroic action was drawn closely from an actual event I had witnessed. It was the story of an extraordinarily courageous officer. The officer was a Jew. But when I came to write it, I automatically changed him to a non-Jew. Deep in my senses was the conditioned, unthinking belief that Jews

were without courage. Then the truth—
something very deep—came to me.
Courage, or the lack of it, is the
property of all men. Neither knows any
boundaries of race or creed. Five years
after I wrote the first version I rewrote it
and Ensign Schiff, the Jew, took his
place at the wheel of the submarine in
that terrible ordeal, bringing his craft
ashore. In that experience I saw my own
anti-Semitism clearly, and in that
experience, I lost it forever.

Goodrich does accept an author's responsibility for three vigorous opinions which he
repeatedly states in his own words, not
those of his characters. (1) His contempt for
politicians who meddle in military affairs is
savage. (2) He consistently favors the decent, hard-fighting Muslim Moros of the
south over the petty, conniving Christian
Tagalogs of the north, as did all American
military men stationed in the Philippines.
And (3) like writers and artists around the
world, he lambastes Protestant clergymen,
especially missionaries like the insufferable
Tiglath Posner, while making sentimental

heroes of Catholic priests like the Irish monk. This is an occupational hazard of novelists, dramatists, motion picture makers and television producers, for the simple reason that Protestant clergymen, with their wives and bawling children, cannot be heroic, whereas priests, with their celibate dedication and attractive garb indubitably are.

I was impressed anew by the grace with which machinery is described, symbolized and used. The United States is a nation in love with mechanics, and it is remarkable that we have produced so few novels which capitalize on this addiction. *Delilah* is one of the best:

> He and most of his men, like their forefathers, were part of a nation that from the very beginning had sought the realization of its dreams through machines. In its homes, on its farms, in its cross-roads stores were machines. It had filled the air and the roads with them, the surface of the sea and its depths. . . . Its poets had found beauty in the precise flight of telegraph wires

across the sky, and the senses of its people first awake to the singing, the odours and the symmetries of machines.

From the moment *Delilah* appeared, critics both praised the poetry of the book and condemned its flowery over-writing. I read this time with special attention to this problem and found a score of stunning sentences for every one that faltered and fell apart. In the first paragraph appears a marvelously brief, sharp description of the ship: "She ate great quantities of hunked black food, and vented streams of grey debris." (Every author worth his salt spells that word *grey*; every editor changes it to *gray*. I have lost this battle a hundred times and I am delighted to see that Goodrich won his. *Grey* is a different word, a different color; it carries a different connotation, a different ring of poetry.) The area occupied by the Moros is "that land so bloody, gaudy and strange."

The bad sentences can be either infelicitous: "Torpedo-tube Number One . . . like a lengthy, grey womb, ever harboured one of the polished steel seeds consecrated to her

254

deadly fertility." Or too clever: "They had travelled far up the blind alley of intimate enmity and friendship ineluctable." Or downright chaotic: "The Swimming Party, nakedly enjoying an illusion of relief from the heat in a liquid whose temperature provided little contrasts to the heavy, incandescent air, an illusion that permitted wild expenditures of energy impossible on the shore, surged continuously back and forth in exuberant factions between the end of the dry dock's floor and the water."

I judge that one exquisite passage, like that dealing with the tower at Aigues Mortes, exculpates the sentences that fail. Unless a writer is trying for those great, singing passages he won't stumble into the bad ones, and repeatedly this book offers paragraphs that explode with poetic imagination. One must conclude that the novel succeeds in most of what it tries.

(5)

Yet for a fellow writer to consider the case of *Delilah* is to experience the heart-break of our profession. In the original edition, on the page facing the opening Chapter I, the author injudiciously but daringly announced that *Delilah* "was the first of two separate novels concerning its subject." And all of us who read this grainy incandescent book waited hungrily for the sequel.

That was in 1941. Thirty-seven years have passed, and the further adventures of *Delilah* in World War I have not yet appeared. Nor has anything else from the pen of this obviously gifted, dedicated man. It is one of the curious silences of literary history, for remember that his first novel was greeted with hozannahs that fall to few men or women when they publish their first book. If ever a writer was encouraged by his public to take the next step, Goodrich was that man.

Indeed, the hackneyed salesman's phrase, "the long-awaited novel of . . ." could have been used here; usually it is meaningless. The only persons who "await a novel" are the author's spouse who has grown anxious about income, or his editor who has a certain number of slots to fill in the publishing schedule that year. Mostly nobody gives a damn whether a specific novel is written or not, but in Goodrich's case we were all awaiting the sequel.

What happened to cause the delay? I inquired widely about the man for whom I had developed such hearty respect and learned from various sources, including several fine bits of newspaper reporting, that Goodrich had spent the years in and after World War II trying to bring his *Delilah* sequel to a successful conclusion. But reporters who'd had the privilege of inspecting the cubicle in a Richmond, Virginia, walk-up, let me read their accounts of how his messy room was lined with large boxes containing not only Volume Two of *Delilah* but also an incredible three other more-or-less completed novels, which he proposed publishing ahead of Delilah II.

People familiar with the case, and of his self-exile in the Richmond flat, told me they could recall no other major artist in whatever field—novel, stage play, painting, sculpture—who had amassed such a wealth of completed material, most of which could surely be published or produced or sold. I asked what about Van Gogh and Emily

Dickinson, and they said: "But that was in another age, before writers like us tracked down the artist and disclosed to the world his hidden treasures."

When I learned of his death without any one of his four potential masterpieces published, I wrote several careful paragraphs stating my sense of loss and my grief that such a talented man—and a naval writer like myself—should have died with his capstone works never to be finished. It was obvious that I held him and his work in warm and tender regard.

I submitted my essay to Matthew Bruccoli, editor of the series in which sensationally successful one-time novels, which had dropped out of circulation, were being revived. *Delilah* was scheduled to be one of the leading revivals. I have never known what happened next, or who passed about my essay, but one afternoon I received a phone call from Richmond.

"Is this Michener, the writer?"

"I work at it." (That's my invariable reply to such questions.)

"But you're the fellow who has just written that review of my novel?"

"Who is this? What novel?"

"*Delilah*. I'm Marcus Goodrich."

"Are you still alive? I just wrote your obituary. Heard about your death from people in Richmond."

"I'm very much alive. Wanted to tell you that you did a damned fine job. You understood what the book was about." There was a pause, then in a deeper voice: "I'm so grateful you took the trouble. And that the book will get a second life. You've made me very happy."

Yes, this wonderful Navy type who had fought in both World Wars and engaged himself in five stormy marriages, including the heaven-sent one to Olivia de Havilland, was still living on the third floor of an apartment house. He told me he was eighty-one years old, keen of mind and surrounded by four unfinished manuscripts.

In a recent letter he said, "There are weeks on end when I seldom hear my own voice. I write six days a week, and on the seventh attend services at the Episcopal church, after which I go for a walk in some area requiring further research for a manuscript.

"My writing day begins at 7:30 in the morning and if I am at a point of action or exposition I write straight through until one o'clock. I've only got six or seven years left. There is not time for anything else. I now seldom write letters to anyone and no one but rarely ever writes to me. For the most part I've become a hermit."

What do the four incompleted manuscripts deal with? The most enticing, of course, is the second volume of *Delilah*. Of it Goodrich says, "It was written before the first part was published." This means that it has been lying about his room for well over forty years. Why has he not released it?

Goodrich served in both World Wars, in the first as a naval ensign specializing in aviation, in the second as a lieutenant-commander in charge of amphibious landings at such hot spots as Sicily and Okinawa. This latter experience, coming so swiftly upon the publication of *Delilah*, altered his whole manner of looking at life. His equanimity was shattered by the radical differences he detected between the men of World War II and those of *Delilah*. He therefore put aside the polishing of his sequel and returned to the three abortive novels depicting this difference.

He found the going rough. Days and weeks and even months would be spent endeavoring to stipulate the differences and their causes. One of the manuscripts is titled "Malagueña Salerosa," the name of one of the most ingratiating songs ever written in Mexico, or in all of Spanish America, for that matter. This song is a favorite of mine, and the fact that Goodrich is using it as his working title bewitches me. What can he be saying that would justify such an extraordinary title? All we know is that he grew up in Texas with many Mexicans at hand, and that in *Delilah* he used Mexican metaphors several times: the singing, a bullfight, the "dollar Mex" used as standard coinage in the Far East at the time of *Delilah* because of its high silver content.

He has said of "Malagueña Salerosa": "Sometimes when I reread it I feel that I shall have it finished in eighteen months. Then, after a time, I read it again and I know it will take longer. I live under pressure." But he has promised one thing: the second half of *Delilah* will not be published until the other three manuscripts have been perfected.

From things he has said earlier, and especially from comments in a recent letter, we can piece together these meager facts about the sequel: "It is behind me, waiting there in the icebox until the time arrives when the three irresistible, later manuscripts are perfected and I can return to it. If ever I come to believe the time will never arrive when I can get back to achieving a final, complete self-satisfaction for it ... I shall probably burn the manuscript."

The name of the sequel? *Delilah in War*. Its contents? Goodrich has divulged only that Signalman Warrington, the introverted lad from Texas, is not lost. He stands waiting for his cue, and when it comes he plays a very important part in the second volume. A central figure, however, will be Seaman Rowe, whom many readers will have overlooked in the first volume because of his inconspicuous role. It is this reluctant man who will bring *Delilah* to disaster, for he is at the wheel, confused and hesitant, when the crisis arises in which *Delilah* is finally sunk.

Beyond that we know nothing. The odds cannot be good that any one of the three later novels will ever be published, but if the manuscript of *Delilah in War* is salvaged and found to be in near publishable form, there will be many like me who will want to read it.

Even if nothing is found publishable in that third-floor apartment, the name of Marcus Goodrich will survive, both as a fascinating literary enigma and as the author of a rough-hewn classic. *Delilah* was not written; it was carved chunk by chunk from living rock and those critics who acclaimed it back in 1941 knew what they were talking about. It is still good reading, and for the reasons they cited. With an additional third of a century of American literary history at my disposal, I cannot write more perceptively of this book than Lincoln Colcord did when he said in the first flush of enthusiasm: "A serious novel of the sea which easily passes muster as a work of literature."

♦　　♦　　♦

Late in 1991 I received word that Marcus Goodrich had died of heart failure on October 20, 1991, at a convalescent center in Richmond, Virginia. He was ninety-three.

In a recent letter, Goodrich's daughter indicated he did not spend his last years in isolation: 'My father visited us for three or four days every month almost without fail. He and my late husband had a wonderful relationship. My sons were wild about him and introduced him to all of their girls, wives and friends. My walls rang with the arguments and discussions.'

Fortunately, he did not burn the four, still-unfinished manuscripts. They are retained by his descendants, perhaps awaiting an aspiring Conrad or Melville—or Goodrich—for their completion.

Truman Capote

———— ◇ ————

Foreword for Conversations with Capote, *by Lawrence Grobel, published by New American Library in 1985.*

photo by Harvey Wang

Truman Capote

Truman Capote was of tremendous importance to writers like me, for he filled a necessary role in American letters, one from which we profited but which we were ill-equipped to perform for ourselves.

England, which has always found a place for the really outrageous eccentric, provided a theater for the naughty Irishman Oscar Wilde, who gave the world, from the salons of London to the mining camps of Colorado, extravagant entertainment.

I never knew the great French artist-poet-actor-poseur Jean Cocteau, but in the years following 1900, when the ineffable Oscar Wilde died, Cocteau became supreme as the visible artist, the man who delighted in the art of *épater la bourgeoisie*, smacking the middle class in the snoot. Extravagant in physical appearance, exhibitionistic by design, flamboyant in action and word and a superb artist in any medium when he wished to be, he constantly reminded the world that artists were different and that much of their worth stemmed from the fact that they behaved pretty much as they damned well pleased. Cocteau enchanted, bemused and outraged generations of staid French and English and German gentlemen, always to the delectation of the watching world and to the enrichment of those who loved either art or boisterous entertainment. Pompous and self-righteous democracies profit from having men like Jean Cocteau and Oscar Wilde nipping at their heels. They need to be reminded that artists are sometimes outrageously against the grain, that they espouse unpopular causes, that they behave in ways that would be unacceptable to others and that they can have waspish tongues. I've always had a strong suspicion that such artists help keep society cleaned up, aware, on its toes and more civilized than it would otherwise be.

In my time in America we have had three such men—Norman Mailer, Gore Vidal and Truman Capote—and their contributions to our national life have been of inestimable value. Let me illustrate by what happened in the space of five days a few years ago. First, Norman Mailer slugged Gore Vidal in New York, in a public literary brawl which received front-page attention. The next day John Gardner, a worthy addition to the Terrible Trio, gave an interview to the *Washington Post* in which he stated bluntly that he was the greatest master of English since Chaucer and that worthies like John Milton, Ernest Hemingway and a flock of other pretenders of such ilk were crocks of something or other. There were so many similar statements that I called the *Post* to verify that Gardner had actually said these things and they assured me: "He said them, and he was sober."

Then, Truman Capote came into our area to speak at a college, but when he lurched onto the stage at eight that evening he was potted and began by abusing the students in rather colorful language. "Why," he wanted to know, "if you want to be writers, aren't you home writing instead of crowding into this hall to listen to an old crock like me?" At that he staggered about, collapsing at the foot of the podium, from where the harassed head of the English department with two helpers lugged his inert body from the stage. End of lecture.

Reading of these dramatic events at the end of one week, I told my wife: "I feel ninety years old at the tail end of a wasted life. I never took part in the main event. I have no claim to call myself a writer." I was secretly jealous of Mailer, Vidal and Capote. They have borne constant testimony to the fact that they are artists. And they have reminded us that artists often require a special freedom which people in other occupations do not seem to need.

In relation to writers like those who make themselves into public figures, writers like me are much like nonunion members in a work force; we profit from the wage increases gained by the union without being dues-paying members or doing the dirty

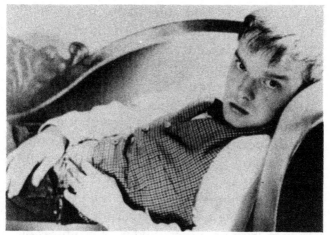

work of running the strike or policing the ranks. We are freeloaders and we know it.

My association with Truman Capote, whom I revered as a man so opposite to myself, began one day in the offices of Random House when Bennett Cerf ran into where I was working, with a copy of that incredible photograph of the young fawn from the Deep South magnolia plantation reclining languorously on a chaise longue. Beneath the famed photo of the sybarite someone had scrawled a play upon the title of the book which had brought Capote fame: *Other Vices, Other Rooms.*

"Look what some son-of-a-bitch sent me!" Cerf bellowed in his high, agitated voice. But then he could not refrain from laughing. "What you need, Michener, is a photograph like this. An attention-getter."

Occasionally thereafter I would encounter Capote in the editorial offices of Random House, and I was present on that hilarious day when it was revealed that another publisher, so much bigger than Random House that it could risk housing its offices in an unfashionable part of New York, had tried to lure Truman into its fold with promises of vast royalties. Cerf bubbled the news: "Capote was tempted, I have to admit that. They offered him a price we couldn't match. But he finally told them in his high, squeaky voice: 'No young man who aspired to be a serious writer would consent to being published by a house which kept its offices west of Fifth Avenue.'"

Sometime thereafter I fell into Bennett Cerf's doghouse by being seen in the bistros of New York with my longtime friend Leonard Lyons, the *New York Post* columnist who had a penchant for artists, musicians and writers. Lyons had publicly accused Cerf of filching items from his column for use in the clever anthologies of wit which he, Cerf, was publishing so regularly and successfully. If I wanted to be friends with Lyons, I could not be friends with Cerf, and vice versa. Although Capote and I were Cerf specials, I met Truman only through Lyons; more important, Lyons also introduced me to a stunning would-be starlet-singer-actress-raconteur from the mines of Montana. She had a minimum talent, a maximum beauty and a rowdy sense of humor. Also, she was six feet, two inches tall, half a head taller than I, a head and a half taller than Truman.

The last point is important, because Truman and I dated her alternately and she was so delightful to be with that I resented it when she accompanied Truman and not me. They made a stunning pair, this statuesque miner's daughter soaring toward the heavens, this rotund little gnome dancing along beside her. It still grieves me to confess that she liked Truman a good deal more than she did me, partly I think because she knew what a striking pair they made, and this was important to a young woman trying to make her way in New York. She also liked Leonard Lyons, because he used her name in his column rather frequently, and she told me one night: "He'll make me the toast of New York." And for a brief spell he did, for she landed a conspicuous television show, and heads turned whenever she strode in like some Amazonian queen with either Capote or me in tow.

Good girl that she was, she never spoke of Truman to me, or of me to Truman, but we had to be aware of the dual game she was playing, and we did not dislike her for it. I was much smitten by her, as was half of New York that year, and I studied her with care, as well as affection, because she was the first real star—I had promoted her to that category although the rest of the world was rather loath to do so—that I had known. Therefore, when Capote's sensationally good *Breakfast at Tiffany's* appeared and a woman in New York threatened to sue Truman because she claimed that the central character, the ineffable Holly Golightly, had been modeled after her, I, in the goodness of my heart, sat down and penned a letter to Random House defending my fellow author. For reasons which will become apparent, I suppose the letter, which I sent to Donald Klopfer, vice-president of the firm, has been destroyed, but I remember well its contents:

Dear Donald:

I cannot sit by and see your friend and mine, Truman Capote, crucified by the lawsuit that hangs over his head. [A nicely garbled metaphor.] The suit brought by the young woman in New York is patently false because I happen to know without question that Truman patterned Holly Golightly after a wonderful young woman from Montana, and if the suit comes to trial, I shall be willing to so testify.

       Jim Michener

Well, the letter had not been in the Random House offices six minutes before Bennett Cerf was on the phone yelling: "Do you have any copies of that crazy letter you sent us?" Before giving me a chance to reply, he added: "Burn them! When I showed Truman your letter he wailed: 'I've been afraid she's going to sue, too.' "

It was obvious to me that Capote had fashioned Holly after the sprightly young woman we both liked so much, but she never sued, mainly because she enjoyed the publicity his book had brought her among her circle of café-society friends, who knew the real situation. But after the near-miss with the lawsuits, Truman saw less and less of her, leaving the field to me, and I continued to be stricken by the girl's bubbling charm. I had to withdraw from the competition, however, because of her intense desire to attract attention.

That was the beginning of a desultory acquaintanceship with Capote, who thanked me for the help I had offered, misguided though it was. I met him occasionally at El Morocco, where he squired Marilyn Monroe, who kicked off her shoes while dancing with him (otherwise she too would have been a head taller).

The more I learned about Capote, the more I liked him. Working with a Hollywood producer, I heard that on cross-country trips, Truman liked to make the driver take him to the library in some rural county seat and wait while he, Capote, ran inside: "First time it happened, I said nothing. Next time I asked: 'Truman, what in hell are you doing in these libraries?' and he explained with childish delight: 'Checking the card catalogs. In this one Mailer had seven cards. Vidal had eight. But I had eleven.'"

Truman invited me to his great bash at the Waldorf, sensation of that season, but I was in Europe, and I believe I never saw him thereafter. After the debacle in Maryland, where he fell drunk before his student audience, I sent him a note which said: "Hang in there, Kiddo. We need you."

I certainly needed him, for as the years passed I grew ever more grateful to him for playing the role of the genius-clown who reminds the general public that artists are always different and sometimes radically so. My last contact epitomized this belief. I had been working diligently on a manuscript in Random House's New York offices—*slaving away* would be a more appropriate term—when I came out of the offices bleary-eyed to find staring at me from the kiosk in the lobby of the building on East Fiftieth Street the stark white cover of a large Greenwich Village newspaper. It contained no title, only a marvelously debauched photograph of my friend Capote—in Spanish sombrero I think, or perhaps it was a nineteenth-century Toulouse-Lautrec opera hat—leering at me, with four stark lines of type upper left:

> I'm an alcoholic
> I'm a drug addict
> I'm a homosexual
> I'm a genius

I acknowledged the first three claims, but the last one gave me trouble. In a rather wandering life I have known personally only two geniuses, Tennessee Williams, who used words and human situations more brilliantly than any of us, and Bobby Fischer, the chess champion, who was geared in some wild unique way. Both men found that to be the vessel housing genius was an intolerable condition and each was destroyed by that burden.

Larry Grobel, the conductor of the interviews on which *Conversations with Capote* is founded, began his extensive sessions with Capote in New York around the same time he was interviewing me in Florida, and I had the rewarding experience of hearing about them and later his reactions to a fellow writer I had long admired. Grobel said flatly that Capote was a genius; his flow of words, always exactly right, came from no common source.

Grobel's judgment forced me to recalculate my estimates of Capote.

At the time of the publication of *In Cold Blood*, I was working in widely scattered parts of the world, and wherever I went *In Cold Blood* was being translated into the local language with all the impact it had had in English. Critics, readers, other writers were all mesmerized by it, and no other book during my productive years enjoyed such popular and critical acclaim.

I judged at the time that Truman must have earned at least four million dollars from his book and more likely five. His extraordinary wealth allowed him to behave in extraordinary manners.

But it was not for his earning that I respected him; it was for his persistence, for the high quality of his work and for his refusal to be downtrodden. I also relished his mastery of the apt quotation, a skill I lack. And, too, I greatly appreciated the way he applied a sentence I had never heard before, even though others claimed that it was an old classic revived for the telling moment. Capote had been coaching his friend Princess Lee Radziwill, Jackie Kennedy's sister, for a dramatic role in a television play, and she had bombed. Consoling her, Capote said: "The dogs bark and the caravan passes on." As one who lived some years among caravans, I was captivated by the felicity of that remark, whether original with Capote or dredged up by him. I think of it a dozen times a year, and I am grateful to him for bringing it to my attention.

Because a good many young people may read this book, I must clarify one point. I liked Capote despite his troubles, and I treasured him as a fellow writer, but I never enshrined him or Oscar Wilde or Jean Cocteau as the ideal writer. Byron was a Truman Capote of his day; Wordsworth and Goethe were not. Most of the world's fine books are

written by ordinary or even drab human be-
ings like Saul Bellow, Anthony Trollope,
Gustave Flaubert, Joyce Carol Oates or
Wladyslaw Reymont, the Polish Nobel laure-
ate. I obviously enjoy Capote but I would
not care to see him replicated endlessly
among our youthful aspirants. He should be
categorized as a later-day Thomas Chatterton, indubitably brilliant, indubitably
incandescent, indubitably doomed.

Is Grobel correct in calling Capote a genius? I'm not sure, because I have stern
qualifications for this word, but I would like
to throw into the critical hopper two bits of
evidence which might support Grobel's con-
tentions.

First, I doubt that any other writer in any
language living at the time of the Kansas
murders could have written *In Cold Blood*
with the severe control that Capote exer-
cised. By that I mean the depiction of an
Aeschylean theme without morose morali-
zing; I mean the choice of precisely the right
vocabulary; I mean the management of ten-
sion and horror without collapsing into ba-
thos; I mean the telling of a highly personal
story—his interaction with two disgusting

murderers—without allowing himself to become a central character; I mean also the pioneering of a new style of novel writing. For all these reasons Capote can be praised for having produced a chilling masterpiece. No one but he could have done it at that time, and few could equal it now.

Second, years later I read with enthralled interest excerpts from Capote's last work, the never-to-be-finished *Answered Prayers*, as they appeared in *Esquire* magazine in 1975 and 1976. I had heard for some years that Truman was at work on what he considered his masterpiece and I had developed a more-than-usual interest. A writer constantly hears that some contemporary is at work on the summon bonum opus which will nail down a secure spot in posterity. Mailer is doing such a work. So is James Baldwin. So is Graham Greene. So is Joyce Carol Oates. So is Otto Defore, whom nobody ever heard of, out in Idaho. So are we all.

But here was Capote actually offering samples from his chef d'oeuvre and I was impatient to sample them. Before I finished the second installment my mind was made up and I recorded my judgment in an aide-mémoire to myself:

A shocking betrayal of confidences, an eating at the table and gossiping in the lavatory. I am familiar with four of the people T.C. lacerates and I can categorically deny the allegations he makes. A masterly study in pure bitchiness which will close many doors previously opened. Why did he do it? Has he no sense of responsibility or no-blesse oblige? A proctologist's view of American society.

But I am sure that if he can bring off the whole, *Answered Prayers* will be the roman à clef of my decade, an American Proust-like work which will be judged to have summarized our epoch. I can visualize graduate students at Harvard in the year 2060 getting their Ph.D.s in literature by deciphering who Capote's more salacious and infamous characters were and then assessing the justice of his comments. The best of these studies, the one that fixes his reputation, will be titled *Truman Capote and His Age*. Like Toulouse-Lautrec, he will come to represent his period, and he will be treasured for the masterly way he epitomized it.

But only if he can finish his work in high style, only if he incorporates enough leading or relevant figures, only if he masters his subject rather than allowing it to overwhelm him. I hear he's drinking so much and into drugs so heavily that the chances of his making it are slim. What will he have left us then? Some fragments to be covered in footnotes. One hell of a lot of would-be literature is compressed into footnotes.

Because of an unusual combination of circumstances, I was allowed to know Capote tangentially and to assess his performance with some accuracy. I had abiding affection for the man and enormous respect for his talent. I envied the classic manner in which he conducted himself and reveled in his public posturing. His quips were first-class, his best writing of high merit, and his *Cold Blood* exceptional in its mastery.

His going leaves a gap. But I would like my permanent salute to him to be what I told him in my last letter: "Hang in there. We need you."

SONNET TO A WEATHERED WANDERER

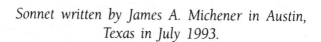

Sonnet written by James A. Michener in Austin, Texas in July 1993.

Sonnet

To a Weathered Wanderer

The day came when he trod our paths
    no more,
His heart was willing but his strength
    declined.
His walking stick stood dusty by the
    door,
And rumor asked: 'Could it be loss of
    mind?'
They sent me to inquire and he
    explained:
'My wandering habit was ordained at
    birth.
'Grieve not for me that now I am
    enchained,
'The mind that soars cannot be bound
    to earth.

'Proust from his bed probed Paris day
 and night,
'While in his garret Chatterton wove
 schemes.
'Milton saw wonders though deprived
 of sight;
'And Emily fled Amherst in her dreams.
 'Imagination roams at little cost,
 'And visions once perceived are never
 lost.'